How Your Senses Control Your Mind

Shirley Northcliff

How Your Senses Control Your Mind
Northcliff Christian Books
733 Tuscany Way
Edmond, OK 73034
snorthcliff059@gmail.com

ISBN: 978-0-692-14693-4

Contents

Dedication

I would like to dedicate this book to all those who have suffered from loneliness, anxiety and have allowed it to consume their lives so much that they shut down the most important parts of their body that keeps them connected to the world around them.

I know from firsthand experience that it is easy to get into a dark hole of despair. Getting out of that shut-down mold is impossible without help.

By sharing with you what God has taught me about my senses, I can show you that we have the power within ourselves to overcome the emotional overload that isolates us from people and takes away our ability to enjoy the wonderful world God has created.

My heart also goes out to all of you that have taken care of an Alzheimer's parent or loved one. This is one of the most difficult things you will ever do in your life, but afterwards you will never regret doing it.

Through this time, if you use your senses to connect with God, He will hold your hand and help you through it. Your reward will be knowing you did everything humanly possible for the person you loved, and you will have a satisfaction you will never loose and no one will be able to take from you.

I would also like to thank Carolyn Marshall, Francie Officer and Fred Hein for taking their time to help with the reading of my book and making the needed corrections.

Review

Shirley Northcliff, in *How Your Senses Control Your Mind*, has given us a refreshing perspective on the use of our five senses (with the relationship of an often-ignored sixth sense added in), especially how we fail to utilize the senses to their fullest potential and, as a result, have allowed them to fall out of use, become out of balance with each other and, most importantly, diminish our overall relationship with God and all of the ways in which He wants us to relate to Him and to the people around us. The hard-hitting, no-nonsense approach she sets forth in this book is a quick and pleasant read but is packed with suggestions on how to conduct a realistic examination of ourselves and how easily our senses are dulled by the constant onslaught of distractions from the world around us and the workings of evil to throw us out of balance and, in the process, throw up a blockage of the intimate fellowship with Him that God desires for us. I believe it will be impossible for anyone to come away from reading the insights Shirley has written down without finding several areas of their own lives which need to be brought into balance.

Fred L. Hein

Forward

This book is designed to help Christians realize that our connection with God, and life itself, is done through our senses.

The brain does not control our life, our senses do. The brain is our hard drive when compared to a computer, the place where our reaction to our senses is stored.

Those of you who do not believe in God may want to stop right here and put the book down. Your perspective of God is that He is a supernatural power that dominates people and zaps them if they do something wrong. God is something religious people have made up to get you to do what they want. That a good loving God wouldn't send anyone to hell. That life is what you make it and when you die there is nothing else. It's all over.

Suppose you had a boss who, every time you went to him/her, made you feel safe and important just being in his presence. That every question you asked was important and meaningful. Who loved you no matter what you looked like or said to him.

Who solved all your problems when you listened to him and did what he suggested. Who willingly took over the situation when you didn't have the strength or power to do it on your own. Who gave you joy, happiness and contentment whenever you obeyed him. Who had the power to comfort you no matter the situation. Who engulfed you with love when life overwhelmed you.

Would you go to that boss at every opportunity or would you rather do it on your own because you want to remain in control of your life.

If you want a boss like the one I described and are tired of trying to do everything on your own, then you need God. That is how He responds to us whenever we have a problem.

Since we are such a visual society we find it hard to believe in something we can't see. Even though we cannot see God, we can feel His presence and we can connect with Him through our senses. In this book I hope to introduce you to your senses and how God intended for us to use them to connect with Him thereby giving us the power to overcome the emotional setbacks we find hard to fight during our life time.

Introduction

For God has not given us the spirit of fear, but of power, and of love, and of a sound mind.

2 Timothy 1:7

In grade school we learned that the five senses where <u>touch</u>, <u>taste</u>, <u>smell</u>, <u>sight</u> and <u>hearing</u>. The teacher discussed the function of each one, but I'm not sure we grasp the importance of them in our life.

I want to introduce you to the five senses, and show you their true purpose and how God intended you to use them together in a complete balance, so we will be able to enjoy life to the fullest.

As I explain the senses, I will give their usual use and then what God has shown me, and how their use affects the mind.

This following information is what I found on the Internet about our senses: *Our five senses are our connection to the outside world. They send messages to our brain which interprets the messages and perceives what is around us. A majority of the information that our senses take in is never recognized by our brain. Our experiences, beliefs and culture affect what we notice out of the thousands of stimuli our senses are receiving. Our brains use information it gathers through our five senses, interprets it and perceives the world around us, creating our life experiences.*

The brain does not trigger our senses. Our senses trigger the brain to react. Think about that for a minute. That means we have control of our mind through our senses, so how we use our senses is important to the functioning of our minds.

Your senses trigger the brain to respond, then the brain triggers the body to respond. That response is stored in the mind and reoccurs when the senses are used again and again. We control how we perceive life through our positive or negative responses. When God is the sixth sense, guiding and directing, we have true balance in our lives.

How you use your senses influences how you respond to the world. Life is full of ups and downs. I don't suggest that these will vanish, but that God will offset the trials of life by bringing joy and contentment to your perception of the world.

Our senses are used in a wide range of responses from the simplistic to the extreme. Some responses may be so traumatic that they are pushed far back in our minds where they are forgotten. Sooner or later, the senses will trigger that traumatic memory and cause a response that is not normal; for example, post-traumatic stress syndrome.

In our study of the senses in grade school, we learned what they were and how our brains responds on a small scale. Over the years we may have read the importance of each sense, but never the balance of the senses and how that balance can keep our brain on an even keel avoiding overload.

I'm sure all of us at one time or another has been asked, "Don't you have any sense?" This is usually asked after we have done or said something "dumb" or inappropriate. But what really should be asked is, "Aren't you using your senses?" Our reaction to our senses forms a memory in our mind and triggers an immediate response or a past memory, or both. For example, when you touch a hot surface, it triggers the brain to react to the pain and to pull your hand away. This is almost an immediate response. The actual memory of the burn and pain will be stored in your brain so that when you encounter the heat again, the brain warns the body not to touch it. This is a memory response.

If these responses were not stored in our minds, we would repeat the same process over and over.

When we <u>hear</u> or <u>smell</u> something we don't like, our response is to ignore or respond.

When someone asks us to perform a disagreeable task and forces us to respond, then a bad experience or memory is formed. As like situations are repeated, frustration, anger or bitterness will become a habitual way of responding. An overload of bad responses will eventually build up so much that all our responses will result in anger.

When we rely on the six sense, the Holy Spirit will help us respond in a pleasant manner in which we can release the bad memory or memories and in this way overcome a bad response and prevent an overload. These feelings also endanger our health: physical, mental and spiritual.

This is why it is so important for us to use our senses in line with God. It is the difference between living a life of anger or one of peace.

Sometimes we get stuck in a negative or destructive way of reacting. For example, if you burn your hand, and you yell, stomp, curse, or strike out at someone that could have turned on the fire, this reaction will be stored in your memory along with memories of the burn. When you continue to react in this manner, everything in your life becomes a disaster and you begin to think the world is against you.

If you burn your hand and your response is to ask God for help to take away the pain or to guide you to use something that will ease the pain, your mind will process a much more pleasant reaction and can be stored as such. In the future you will not only know not to touch the fire again, but the memory of how God took charge will come back to mind. Before long the positive responses will replace those "old" negative responses. Unpleasant and hurtful circumstances are no longer a disaster in your life. The more our responses are controlled by God, the better and more positive our life becomes. You will be filled with joy and contentment because your senses are in balance with God. God intends for us to enjoy life!

Excluding abusive situations, we can no longer blame others for what happens in our lives.

Your senses are very special gifts from God

and a way to see life through His eyes. Without your senses you would be like a robot moving through life waiting for voice commands. Instead you were created in His image and given the same abilities to experience everything in life as He does.

God created everything on earth for you to enjoy, and you are to do that through your senses. This may sound repetitive but I want you to grasp the fact that how you respond to your senses is how you respond to the world around you.

Using your senses with God as your sixth sense, you experience and share your whole life with Him, in pleasure, joy, peace, love, confidence and contentment.

When your senses are not used in balance or under God's guidance and protection, the devil seeks to destroy you with worry, anxiety, and fear, which often results in depression and Alzheimer's.

There have been, and still are many professionals that do extensive studies of the brain and how it works. My perception of the six senses will in no way contradict their studies. I am not a psychiatrist or a physician and certainly would not discourage using their services.

As you walk with me through these chapters, I will show you how to properly use your senses, enabling you to experience life fully and enjoy God's Special Gifts, your six senses: **<u>taste, smell, sight, hearing, touch and God.</u>**

CHAPTER ONE

Touch

Rev. 3:20 KJV

Touch is an important sense because it not
only performs a body function to protect us, it connects us with others. It is one of the most important
sense of all because it can affect the other senses. If
we isolate ourselves from people, we not only shut
down our sense of touch, but we also shut down our
other senses that could connect us to the outside
world as well.

We all need to be held and touched. A (Christian) touch connects us with God.

Before I explain what I mean let's look at what
the Internet says about touch: *The sense of touch is
spread through the whole body. Nerve endings in the
skin and in other parts of the body send information
to the brain. There are four kinds of touch sensations*

*that can be identified: cold, heat, contact, and pain. Hair on the skin increases the sensitivity and can act as an early warning system for the body. The fingertips have a greater concentration of nerve endings. (People who are blind can use their sense of touch to read Braille – a kind of writing that uses a series of bumps to represent different letters of the alphabets.)**

So with touch, we feel cold, heat, contact, and pain. We're all born with these sensations. We learn from our parents how to react to these nerve endings and the sensations they cause. When we got cold, they wrapped us in a blanket or turned on the heat to soothe that uncomfortable feeling. When we were hot, they did something to cool us. When we got older, we were taught not to touch things that are hot because it will cause pain. These responses are stored in our memory and will resurface when needed throughout our life. Our senses are the source in which our brains grow and develop.

Touch forms emotions. Love is the very first emotion we feel when the nurse puts us in our mother's waiting arms. This is when we first experience the nerve endings in our bodies and how good it feels to be held in a loving manner. We not only feel love but we have a feeling of being safe and content. These emotions are stored in our brain and will resurface each time we are held in a warm caress. This is our first experience of love and it is such a strong emotion because it comes from God. It will be stored in our mind and never leave us. We will long for it throughout our lives.

Studies have proven that if children are never hugged or loved with contact from their parents they may be withdrawn from people the rest of their lives. Empathy may never develop in their life because it is not a stored memory in their mind. If parents never sympathized with their pain as a child, they will more than likely never feel sympathy for others.

Pain is a part of our sense of touch that we will do anything to avoid. When we feel pain from a physical contact, our sense of touch will trigger the brain of pain and our brain will trigger the body to respond in a way that will defend you from further pain. That's how we know to fight. We learn at an early age that we were born and some day will die, but until that day comes we have an instinct to survive. We understand self-defense and we learn at that early age to avoid physical pain. Emotional pain can be more of a struggle in our life because we come into contact with it every day.

Our hearts not only pump the blood supply to our bodies but it also sends emotional responses to our brains. The heart is the one part of the body that we protect the most because if it stops beating we know our life is over. No wonder God has control over when it starts and stops. Only God. The amazing thing though is that God gives us the opportunity to let Him protect us from evil and will give us unconditional love and show us how to use it in our life when we accept His Son as our Savior from sin and evil. Revelation 3:20 KJV says: *Behold, I stand at the door and knock: if any man hear my voice, and open the door, I will come in to him, and will sup with him, and he with me.*

God is love and every emotion associated with that: joy, peace, contentment, patience, kindness, goodness, faithfulness, gentleness and self-control.

The devil is the opposite of God and possesses hate and every emotion associated with that trait: anger, fear, worry, pain, anxiety, misery, hatefulness, conniving, self-absorbed and out of control evil. The devil is the true meaning of narcissism: love of one's self.

God gave man free-will because we were made in His image. He wanted man to choose to love Him. God never forces Himself on anyone. God doesn't possess the desire to control you because there is no one above Him. He doesn't have to prove He is worthy to be served because He is. He is the great I am. He has the desire to love and be loved as He loves. He is all there is, but He still wants to be loved as He loves. Without conditions. When there is no one greater, there is no need for negotiation.

When you turn your life over to God you never feel like you have lost your identity. You know that you are a part of a huge entity. Life is no longer about me, me, me, anymore. It's all about God. God is the ultimate being. The reason for existing, your purpose, and the more you will yourself to God the more you become like Him. The essence of love is God.

Because of Adam and Eve's disobedience to God they were cursed and cast out of the Garden of Eden. Their life changed because they now knew the devil and all he consisted of. They became aware of 'self' which they could choose to serve just as the devil was doing. Before they ate of the 'Tree of Knowledge,' they were as 'one with God.' Everything that He had, which was good, was theirs for the taking. They not only could see God but because of their senses being like His, they could experience fully and enjoy everything He created. After partaking of the forbidden fruit, they knew everything evil as well. Now the devil had access to their senses, and because of this, what we do with our senses is a struggle between right and wrong. We must choose God.

God wants unconditional love and obedience, not because He is King but because He is the essence of Love. He is everything that is good. He doesn't want us to suffer and struggle through life. He wants us to have a balance (complete total awareness) of our senses so we are in tune with Him as He had intended man to be in the first place. Remember our senses are how our minds perceives life. When you accept God through His son who died for our sins, we die to 'self' and the Holy Spirit becomes our Sixth Sense that gives us directions on how to live our life and fill our senses with all He still has to offer us today. When you use all your senses to touch God, He is able to be as one with you. You become everything that is good and the devil has no control over you.

Touch is so important in everyday life as well. God doesn't just touch our hearts when we allow Him in, He embraces our hearts and engulfs us with love. The love He gives us is not to be hidden or stored away for only us to enjoy when we want it. He wants us to share it with everyone. We never lose love by giving it away. We gain even more because we receive love back. The more love you give, the more you get back. It's when you start hoarding that love and try to keep it for yourself that you start losing love. You become self-absorbed and think your love is only yours. Everything becomes all about you. This is how the devil distorts love and begins a spiraling destruction of your life.

Loneliness is an increasing problem in the world today but not necessarily because we have no one to talk to.

Years ago there was a big issue about marriages breaking up because of lack of communication. Communication, communication, communication was all people talked about. So communication became everyone voicing his/her opinion, but no one was listening.

Lack of talking is definitely not an issue today. The problem is that no one is listening. Communication is an equal balance of talking and listening on both sides.

Talking is not lacking in our lives today, but touching is. Marriages are breaking up because couples aren't touching. When we touch, we share needed emotions that add depth to our relationships.

The first thing we want to do when someone says something that hurts our feelings is to run. The last thing we want to do is touch them or be touched.

When you try to communicate with someone who doesn't want to listen, you should gently touch them on the hand or shoulder to get their attention.

(We all long to be touched in a loving manner.) Do not grab them or violate them in any way because this kind of touch triggers the brain not to respond. You cannot get your point across by using violent measures.

If you and your spouse have something difficult to talk about, you should sit at a table and hold hands while you talk. This triggers the brain to respond in a lucid manner because you can feel the love from one another. Speak in a calm loving manner even if it is criticism. Never accuse or raise your voice when trying to communicate. We respond better when we know we are loved.

When you work in the public you will come across difficult people from time to time. I found that if you touch them gently on the hand, arm or shoulder and give them a compliment they completely change their attitude. You connect with that person from your touch.

Many times they are going through something difficult in their life and they take it out on the people around them. Never take them personally and let them upset you. Remember they don't know you at all. Give them what God gives us, love and understanding.

If you have the love of God in you, it will touch them through you. God can work through us and He can soften their hearts, something words alone cannot do. The sense of touch is such a positive way of communicating.

I heard a story about a woman that was waiting

in line at a grocery store. There was an older lady in front of her and she saw that the tag on her blouse was sticking out, so she reached up and gently tucked the tag back under her blouse. The older lady started crying and the woman said, "Oh, I am so sorry did I hurt you?" She said, "No, you didn't hurt me, it's just that I haven't been touched in so many years. Thank you."

The older lady wasn't hurt; she longed to be touched.

One of the worst things we can do is to isolate ourselves from people. We need the human touch. When we deprive ourselves of touching or being touched we deprive ourselves of love.

We cannot have a balance in our lives if we don't touch. When we shut down the sense of touch we force our other senses to work harder. Over a long period of time this can cause an overload on our brains.

When an electrical circuit overloads it blows a switch. Our brain does the same thing.

When God touches our hearts and we allow the Holy Spirit to control our lives, then God is in us. We become as one with Him. John 17:21 KJV: *That they may be one; as thou, Father, art in me, and I in thee, that they also may be one in us: that the world may believe that thou hast sent me.*

When we believe Jesus is the same as God and accept him in our hearts, God takes charge and control of our lives to bring us a kind of love that in the world, we could never obtain or possess. It is an unconditional love that will never leave us.

The devil can no longer possess this love so he in turn tries to possess us. That is why it is so important to turn from the world. The world the devil has taken charge of and rules. A world filled with hate that will consume and destroy you.

The devil cannot feel love so he does not want us to touch others.

God works through us. When He is in control of our lives, it touches others and makes them want what we have; a love that surpasses all human understanding.

The devil has caused so much turmoil in the world with hate, confusion, disease, isolation, self-absorption. He uses any tool he can to keep us from feeling God. He doesn't want us to be as one with God because then God could use us as His vessel to reach others.

The devil does not want us to become soldiers for God, bringing all that is God to people in the world that are confused and hurting. That would defeat his purpose and destroy his plans.

The devil's desire is to be ruler, the one that everyone would bow down to. He is the extreme narcissist.

The definition of a narcissist is: *A person that is excessively preoccupied with personal adequacy, power, prestige and vanity, mentally unable to see the destructive damage they are causing themselves and to others in the process.*

So the devil is the extreme opposite of God. When God cast him from heaven, he became the ruler of the world. The one that would bring the opposite of everything God is.

He has no love of any kind. Just the extreme desire to be served and worshipped, giving nothing in return except what he is; walking, talking destruction. The devil uses the tongue more than anything because he wants to tear down your spirit.

You hear people today talking about trying to find themselves. They want to find out who they are and what their purpose in life is. They spend lots of money and valuable time searching for themselves. (Which by the way is making people more and more self-absorbed.) That is just plain crazy.

The devil is keeping you in turmoil. You are going round and round in a circle like a dog chasing his tail.

You're isolating yourself from others because everything becomes about you in self- preservation.

You cling to everything that is about you because that is who you are searching for. You possess the same thing the devil does, narcissism.

What we need to be searching for is love and allowing God to process our lives. When He has control of our hearts and lives we reach out to others and He can touch them as well. There is no chasing the tail. We continue on in an organized line, from beginning to end. God is alpha and omega. The beginning and the end.

You don't have to find yourself because you are not lost anymore. You know who God is so you therefore know who you are. The essence of Him. You have no desire to become God because He gives you all that you could possibly need. He is not a selfish God. He is a loving God that touches us and allows us to touch Him.

In churches today people are shying away from shaking hands, holding hands, and hugging because they are afraid of getting some sort of germ. They are living their lives afraid of getting sick.

We have to remember that God is in us and God does not get sick. If you are afraid to touch others because you do not want to get sick then you need to plead the blood of Jesus over your heart and not allow the devil to bring these illnesses to you.

God is in control and He must work through us. Because of our faith we possess many blessings from God, and when you possess these blessings they are stored in your mind. By touching others God can work through you and use your faith to touch others.

If you have reassurance from God, you can transfer that reassurance to others by touching them in a loving, compassionate manner.

If they feel isolated from life you can bring them a sense of love just by your hug.

If they have little confidence, you can give them confidence by touching them. Your confidence enters them.

If they feel unimportant, that no one cares if they are there, your touch will assure them that they are important and that you are glad they exist.

The devil works overtime on our minds and the stored images we have of ourselves. The sense of touch can take all the doubt away and erase those old memories and worries from our mind.

We in essence give love to others by touching them. The love that God fills our heart with is transferred to them by a mere hug. **(Do not stop touching.)**

God touches us every day. We must share that blessing with others. Go out and hug someone. It will make you feel good.

I am a hairstylist and I hug everybody before they leave. My people are so used to that hug that they will not leave without it. Sometimes they come back to me before they get out of the door, even if I have hugged them, because they can't remember if I hugged them or not. I hug them again.

A hug is a physical way of letting people know that you love them. It is the one gift for which you get something back in return.

If you come across a person that does not want to be touched, you need to start out touching them gently on the shoulder or hand. They probably have not been touched much in their life and carry a feeling of rejection with them everywhere they go. Never force yourself on someone, remember, do not violate them. You have to teach them to get rid of those old stored feelings of rejection in their mind and replace them with the love and compassion of God. Over a period of time they will become accustomed to touch and will begin to long for it.

Do not take it as rejection when someone doesn't want you to touch them. It is because of what they have stored in their mind that causes such a reaction, it's not anything to do with you.

The closer you get to God the more everything is about Him and not about you. Let Jesus be your example and reach out, touch and show God's love.

We must understand that we connect to God through our senses.

God is not emotions. Emotions are the reaction to our senses. When we live our life through our emotions we are actually living in past responses to our senses.

When God touches our hearts and we accept Him into our lives, our emotions become His feelings or emotions: love, joy, acceptance, safe, confidence, contentment and happiness. The old emotions of the devil: unloved, scared, rejected, unhappiness is no longer a part of us.

Before knowing God, we had a feeling of not belonging anywhere. When God touches our lives, we no longer have a need of finding ourselves because we have found the one who designed us. We have a feeling of being found because we belong to Him.

The devil will offer you the world and make you think the more you have in the world the better off you will be. That more will bring you happiness. Happiness with the devil is fleeting, because he works on your emotions.

The devil no longer has a connection to God through his senses. He can only give you past responses he once had when he was a part of God. That is why the world can never make you feel safe because the devil knows he is no longer safe. He is destined to be destroyed.

When you are a part of the world you are a part of the devil's emotional roller coaster, searching and searching but never finding. You become addicted to your emotions. Self becomes so important to you that you will do anything to feel just a little bit of happiness.

If you think in terms of God being contentment and the devil happiness you can understand how people get addicted to so many things in this world. Happiness from the devil is fleeting. So you search and search for anything that will make you happy. When it doesn't last, you reach for more and more.

When you are addicted to being happy, you start craving anything that will give you a thrill. The thrills you seek will give you an adrenaline rush that will turn you into an adrenaline junkie. You live your entire life for that rush with no concern of consequences.

When you know the Lord and He touches your life, you will seek to please Him. When you please and honor God, He will reward you with a feeling of contentment that will never leave you. Contentment from the Lord is ever-lasting.

The reason the devil can only bring you happiness for a short time is because he doesn't have the power to control your heart, so he concentrates on your emotions. Remember emotions are only reactions to your senses.

When God doesn't control your senses, the devil uses your emotional responses against you. He will fill your mind with worthless emotions.

You'll get bombarded with so many emotions you will be unable to sort through them. Your mind will be unable to store them properly and you will become overwhelmed. This overload will cause stress and anxiety that takes over your life. You'll find it hard to make sense of anything and start piling on negative emotion on top of negative emotion until you have a mountain of uncontrollable responses in your memory bank.

This may cause you to shut down your senses and isolate yourself from people. You stop feeling anything because you shut down the five senses that connect you with others and God. The further away you get from God the less you feel.

Extreme cases of this shutdown are self-mutilation. They have gotten so far away from God that they can't feel anything. They cut themselves just to feel. What a horrible way to live.

Without our senses our brains have nothing to react to. We have no emotions and we feel nothing at all.

It is so important that we never allow our emotions to control our lives, or depend on them so much that we forget what our senses are and how they are to be used to connect with God.

Society is on an emotional roller coaster. Up and down, round and round. They are not using their senses in a positive way to connect with God. They are searching for the next thrill. They do nothing to store the mind with good, lasting contentment that can be tapped into at any time to restore their soul. They search and respond to only those things that bring them happiness for the moment.

They taste, smell, touch, hear and see only those things that give them a happy response, what makes them feel good.

"If it feels good do it," is many people's philosophy without any regards to consequences. Their only goal and purpose in life is to make themselves feel good. They allow their senses to try anything. They ignore bad emotions and search for those that bring the kind of happiness that can only come from the world.

The world is full of darkness and soon it will engulf them. They lose all sense of reality and do whatever it takes to bring them a small moment of happiness. In the process they lose all connection to others and God.

John 8:12 KJV says: *Then Jesus spoke saying: "I am the light of the world; he who follows Me will not walk in darkness, but will have the light of life."*

We must use our senses to connect with God or we will lose our life to the darkness of the world.

CHAPTER TWO

Taste

*T*aste is the one sense that we are aware of using more than any of our senses. It is important to our daily living because without food our body will not survive.

Let's first see what the Internet says about taste: *Our sense of taste comes from the taste buds on our tongue. These buds are also called <u>papillae</u> (puh-pih-lee). But, the sense of smell also affects our sense of taste.*

The tongue is only able to taste four separate flavors: salty, sweet, sour, and bitter. You may wonder how different sweet foods taste differently if there are only four flavors. That is because a combination of sweet and salty could be your favorite candy. And the combination of sweet and bitter could be the chips in your chocolate chip cookie. Everything you taste is a combination of these four flavors.

When we taste something that is familiar to us it triggers the brain and brings up a memory of eating it before. It may be a good memory, or a bad memory if you didn't like the way it tasted.

The taste buds give us the ability to enjoy the texture, consistency and flavor of our food. Our fast-paced lives many times interferes with our enjoyment of this sense.

Instead of sitting down at a table and enjoying the pleasure of eating, we find ourselves eating while we are driving, reading, talking on cell phone, texting, working on computer, etc. We are multi-tasking, depriving our mind of making a pleasant experience of eating.

Multi-tasking sends many different signals to our minds. Our minds may not recognize that we ate because of the many tasks we are performing with our other senses. Whatever task is most important to you will take precedence over eating and be stored as such in your mind.

Doing other things while we eat may cause us to over eat because we have not stored the memory of eating.

If God meant for us to keep busy while we ate, He would not have given us taste buds that allow us to savor the food and store the memory of it in our brain as a peaceful, enjoyable part of our day.

You probably never thought of eating bringing you joy and peace. We all desire peace and long for joy in our lives but we do everything to jumble up the signals to our brains that are designed to do just that.

I once dated a guy that enjoyed eating out.

He didn't cram food in his mouth, he savored every moment of it. He simply enjoyed every aspect of it. Tasting everything as though it was something precious. Something he wanted to remember long after he had eaten. It wasn't weird at all.

When he enjoyed something he tasted, he would tell me how good it was and offer me a bite. He used his knife to gently pick it up and place it on my fork and let me taste it. We didn't just eat food, we dined. I think that is what God had in mind.

Some of our best memories of eating are when we have been in a special place that has good atmosphere, quiet so we can talk comfortably. We sometimes discuss the food after smelling the great aroma. We can look around and see and hear others enjoy the meal. We might even touch hands or brush shoulders lightly as we enjoy our food and conversation.

So what have we done? We have used all our senses, therefore a balance that will be stored in our memory as pleasant.

In our busy lives we find ourselves rushing to a restaurant. We hurry everyone in so we can get a seat and not have to wait then instantly look around to find the waiter or waitress to take our order. Complain if they aren't there immediately.

While we wait, we grab our cell phones and check our messages or play a game. Yell at the kids if they get fidgety while tapping our foot complaining how long it is taking to get our food.

Then when we get our food, we examine it and complain about how it looks, how it is cooked, and exclaim how cold it is.

This kind of behavior must really disgust God. We have used all of our senses in such a manner and in turn stored a memory in our mind that repeats itself over and over again. Instead of looking forward to eating we find it a challenge.

God designed us to be dependent on Him, and eating is an example of that dependency. If we don't eat we will die. But just like with all our other senses, He wants to share that experience with us. When we allow God to be a part of our meal time we will enjoy every aspect of it.

As Christians we pray and thank God for what He has given us. We acknowledge His presence in our lives and give Him credit for the many good things He has given us that day. Why not invite Him to dine with us? Isn't that a wonderful concept?

The first thing He invites us to do when we die and go to Heaven is to *'Come and dine.'* He is looking forward to dining with us in Heaven at the great celebration dinner. Why shouldn't we enjoy having Him with us here every day, every meal?

The more we share our lives with God, the more the chaos of this world will disappear. Order will take place in our lives.

Studies have shown that families that sit at a table and eat their meals together have a closer relationship. When we have a pleasant dining experience with others, we have tasted, smelled, seen, heard and touched. If God was there with us, we completely enjoyed our eating experience with all our senses. We had balance.

CHAPTER THREE

Smell

Smell is an important part of memory. It will either register an old memory or store a new memory if you have never smelled the item before.

Before we get into explaining the importance of smell, let's look at the definition of smell: *The nose is the organ that we use to smell. The inside of the nose is lined with something called the mucous membranes. These membranes have smell receptors connected to a special nerve called the olfactory nerve.*

Smells are made of fumes of various substances. The smell receptors react with the molecules of these fumes and then send these messages to the brain. The sense of smell is capable of identifying seven types of sensations. These are put into these categories: camphor, musk, flower, mint, ether, acrid, or putrid. The sense of smell is sometimes lost for a short time when a person has a cold.

In addition to being the organ for smell, the nose also cleans the air we breathe and impacts the sound of our voice. Try holding your nose and talking. Smell is also an aid in the ability to taste.

Have you ever smelled something so good that you could taste it?

Have you peeled an apple and salivated out of the anticipation of how you know it is going to taste? This is because the smell of the apple triggers the memory in our brain to how it tasted in the past. Our minds are full of such past memories.

When we lose the sense of smell or get too busy to enjoy the aroma, we are cheating ourselves out of pleasant memories. Not only that, but we are shutting down past memories. (I read once that people who lose their sense of smell will probably end up with Alzheimer's).

Smell is of course important to breathing and provides air to the lungs and brain. It is part of our bodies' makeup and functions. It's a necessity of life and we are fully aware of our need for it.

Smell can also warn us of danger. The smell of smoke reminds us of the danger of fires.

Foul smells of food trigger our brains not to eat it. Any unpleasant odor will trigger a past memory that alerts us to react in a way that will protect us.

We have a tendency to associate a certain smell to individuals because our memory bank has stored in our minds how they usually smell.

Shampoos, soaps, perfumes or lack thereof, are stored in our minds and we learn to associate those smells with people who use the same product all the time.

When someone you know wears a different perfume or aftershave, our brains becomes alert to the fact that something is different.

If it is something we don't like, our brains will file it in our memory's bank as bad. Even if we never tell the person, our memory banks will recall it in our minds and will recognize it if they wear it again, or anyone else for that matter.

Smell gives depth to the things we see. A rose becomes much more beautiful once we smell its sweet fresh scent. Food tastes better because of the aroma it gives off while cooking. Air becomes fresher when it rains.

When we concentrate more on what we like about objects, we store more pleasant memories in our mind instead of bad.

When we associate a smell with that memory, then every time we inhale it, a complete visual of things in the past will surface in our minds. For example: When I smell fried chicken cooking, my mind pulls up a vision of mother standing in front the stove turning the chicken as it sizzled.

I'm peeling potatoes and my sister is helping mother with the apple pie that is ready to come out of the oven. Or putting the bread in the oven as my dad, brothers and our spouses sit around the table talking and laughing.

Daddy might be telling stories of his childhood or one of the boys reminiscing about something that happened in their childhood.

It almost plays out as a movie in our minds because during those visits we could see, hear, smell, touch each other from time to time because the room was small and so many people were there.

The food smelled so good we could almost taste it before it was placed in front of us. Not only was my sense of smell used, but all my senses were in balance.

The sense of smell is the one sense that often brings up the complete visual memory. I can see a chicken and not think of Sunday dinner. I can see and hear people laughing and talking and not think of it. I can be in a crowded room touching people as I try to pass and not think of it. I can even taste chicken and not think of it, but the smell of it frying brings back the total memory because it triggered all my senses that were used that day.

Or could it be we only get visual memories when all our senses are used in unity. (Balance)

I feel we get more memories from smell because we have a tendency to not inhale things that are bad.

Our minds put things that smell bad or can hurt us in a file that says, "no" when we have an option to sniff it. Our minds will say do not touch, taste, look or listen. We can shut down all of our senses by a simple whiff of something we don't want to smell.

We don't always get an option to see or hear what we want, because it can be forced on us without realizing it until it is too late. People very seldom force you to smell something. We have more control over what we smell; therefore, we have more good memories with our sense of smell.

As we get older we get lazy about smell. We

just rely on past memories of how it smelled or we ignore it completely.

When we actually make a point of smelling, it revives all our senses. You feel refreshed or renewed.

Even though you know how something smells, to actually sniff it will rejuvenate you and ignite your memory process. Just that renewed sniff could clear your mind of negative thoughts and bring back a positive reaction to something as routine as eating a simple apple or peach.

I can smell a peach and automatically think of the peach orchards in Stratford, close to where I was raised. The owners of the orchards would let us go in and pick the peaches for ten dollars a bushel. The sweet and pleasant odor radiated throughout the fields. It is a wonderful memory I will always cherish.

Just eating a peach does not bring back my memories, but when I take the time to smell it, the memories come flooding in. I'm sure that is where we get the saying, "stop and smell the roses." You can walk by rose bushes a hundred times a day and recall in your mind how they smell, but when you stop and take a sniff, you truly enjoy the rose and the memories it brings to mind.

I do everything fast. I don't know why exactly. Maybe I feel there is so much to do and so little time to do it. My husband would tell me to slow down, 'take time to smell the roses.' I'd laugh and say, "I can smell a lot more roses as fast as I go."

The truth is I didn't. I saw a lot of roses, but

never took a whiff of one.

Thank God I do now, and by doing so I connect with Him more. I enjoy every aspect of the rose the way He intended for me to do. By doing so I also enjoy the creator of that rose.

I can not only bring back memories, but I am making new ones that will last me into my latter years.

When you smell something, it is either a new memory or an old memory. If you have smelled it before your mind will recall all you know about it and help you decide if you like it or not.

If you did like it in the past, it may bring up a visual of an entire incident and cause it to play out like a movie in your mind. (As I described earlier.)

If you have never smelled something, your mind will alert you it is new. You will examine it and decide if you like it or not. Whatever you decide about the smell will be stored in your mind as good or bad. The next time you smell it, what you decided about it the first time will come back to you as well.

This is why it is important to take time to enjoy the smell of things because if you don't, you won't have much to remember in your past. Good memories from your past will brighten a sad day in the present.

CHAPTER FOUR

Sight

*Now then, stand and see this great thing the
Lord is about to do before your eyes!*
1 Samuel 12:16

Sight is the one sense we are most aware of in our lives because we are a visual society. We have a hard time acknowledging things we can't see. We enjoy sight because it paints a picture of everything that is in front of us.

Let's look at sight as the Internet describes it: *Our sense of sight is all dependent upon our eyes. A lens at the front of the eyeball helps to focus images onto the retina at the back of the eye. The retina is covered with two types of light sensitive cells – the cones and the rods. The cones allow us to see color and the rods allow us to see better at night and also aid us in our peripheral vision. All of this information is sent to the brain along the optic nerve.*

The images sent are actually upside down, and our brains makes sense of what it receives by turning the vision from two eyes to create a 3D (three dimensional) image. This allows us to perceive depth.

Some people are not able to tell red colors from green colors. This is called color blindness. Others, through injury or other conditions, have little to no sight at all.

Sight is a special gift from God that is given to us so we can enjoy the earth as He created it. The colors, designs, dimensions, uniqueness and magnitude of everything God has created we can grasp with our eyes.

Sight is the one sense we take for granted and can never be truly appreciated unless you have the misfortune of losing it.

When I was thirty-one I developed a brain tumor on my pituitary gland, which is directly behind the optical nerve. As the tumor grew my sight diminished. At first everything was foggy, and as time passed it became denser and denser. A week before the surgery I couldn't see anything in front of me; it was totally black. My peripheral vision was perfect so I saw light coming in from the sides, which helped me get around, but it was very annoying and caused headaches at times when too much light came in.

When I started losing my sight, my other senses intensified, especially my hearing. Touching things became my sight. Smelling and tasting brought a visual picture to my mind.

Even though I couldn't see, my mind gave me an awareness to everything I did through the senses

I had left. It was an amazing experience, one that I will never forget.

When you lose one of your senses your dependency on God becomes even more apparent.

As a Christian your sixth sense (Holy Spirit) will take control when you relinquish your complete will to God.

Surgery was required to remove the tumor, and the night before it was to take place, a team of doctors and interns came into my hospital room to explain what would be going on the following morning.

Since they would have to go through my nose to get behind the tumor to retract it, my neurologist introduced me to the otorhinolaryngology specialist. (Nose, ear & throat) Of course there had to be an ophthalmologist (eye) specialist to observe the optical nerve.

The introductions to the doctors and to the interns was intimidating enough, but the explanation of what would occur during the surgery was very frightening.

My neurologist began explaining, "Well as I told you the other day, the tumor is located in the center of the brain right behind the optical nerve. Years ago they used to go in from the top of the skull, cut it open, and pick up the brain so they could see the tumor and extract it."

Continuing with a slight pause he said, "We found there were too many complications from disturbing the brain so we started looking for alternative ways to remove it.

"We have found that the nose is the best means, if the nose is big enough. This allows us to go in behind the tumor and extract it.

"If the nose isn't big enough, we can go through the roof of the mouth.

"Our otorhinolaryngology doctor here said your nose will be just fine," pointing to the doctor he was referring to.

He leaned over to explain in more thorough terms and said, "He will make a slice here along the side of your nose, pull the skin over and push the center part of your nose over. Then we will remove the bone that goes from your nose and between the eyes to make a path to get behind the tumor where it is lodged behind the optical nerve. That bone will not be able to be replaced so you will have to be careful from that point on not to get hit between your eyes. Your face would become mush. Also, you will probably never be able to smell anything again because of the disturbance to the membranes."

The doctor held up a small instrument and said, "We will cut a hole into the skull and use this little instrument to suck that tumor out. Since we can't see what we are doing, this instrument has a little camera on it and it will reflect on a screen what we are doing."

"Do you have any questions so far?" pausing a moment to get a breath and to see if I was keeping up with his analyses.

"No," I said, slightly shaking my head.

"Okay, there is one problem though."

"What?" I said, thinking to myself, *'Only one?'*

"When we start sucking out the tumor, if it is attached to the optical nerve whatsoever you will be blind the rest of your life."

"Okay, I'll see you'll tomorrow." I said, nonchalantly.

"Did you hear what I said?" The neurologist exclaimed.

"Yeah, I heard you and I'll see you tomorrow."

The Lord and I had been talking about an hour before they came in and He assured me that He was going to be with me blind or not. I had given it to God completely and I knew He would take care of me, one way or another.

The doctors all seemed so sad as they ducked their heads and left the room. Some were shaking their heads from side to side as they departed. I got the distinct feeling they felt sorry for me, thinking I didn't understand what could possibly happen to me tomorrow.

When I woke up in the recovery room, the light was so bright and all I could say was, "I can see! I can see!"

The nurse came running over and asked, "You can see, honey?"

"Yes, I can see! I can see!" praising God more than talking to anyone in the room.

I saw the nurse's face and she glowed like an angel and I said, "You're sooo pretty."

Laughing, she said, "Honey, you're just glad you can see."

She was so right and I have never taken my sight for granted since. God gave me my sight back and from that point on I have respected it and enjoyed it for the tremendous gift it is from Him.

You may never have to go through what I did, but I hope I can help you appreciate your sight as I do today.

In the world today there is so much to see. Technology has far surpassed anything we could have imagined as a child and it is progressing more rapidly every day. Not only does television reveal anything we could imagine, there is no limit to what we can pull up on the Internet by simply Googling it.

There are neuroscientists and psychologists who study the brain and discover more and more everyday about its ability. They believe only a small fraction of its capability is being used.

I can agree that we have extensive hard drives (brains) when compared to a computer. I wonder though, do our minds do the same thing as a computer when you push too many buttons too fast. Does it at times receive too much information so fast that it can't file it in its proper place.

You can push "Enter" too many times too fast on your computer and lock it up. Do our minds do that? Are we pushing the same button too many times so that our mind can't file it or discard it quick enough?

Are we receiving so much information from our fast-paced world that instead of filing it in our minds, it floats around like spam?

Does it pop up later, in the most inconvenient times, leaving us wondering where it came from?

Do we have trouble getting rid of unwanted information fast enough which prevents our memory banks from working properly?

Are we forcing our emotions to respond too quickly, moving so fast that half the time it doesn't register what we have seen? Is this causing us anxiety? Does it eventually lead to depression and Alzheimer's because we just want to shut down and stop the emotional roller coaster we have gotten on?

Did we get on the ride intentionally or did we just see someone get on and we followed? Are we relying on God to lead us or are we following the crowd?

I believe as Christians we need to depend on God and fill our sight and memory banks with positive beauty that God has provided us with.

I read an article once which said to overcome depressed moods, you should find a view that you truly love. It could be your favorite place in the house, where you can stare out of the window and relax, enjoying the beauty of nature. The column claimed this would clear your mind and refresh you.

Hmmm, so what they are actually saying is slow down. Relax the brain. Enjoy the natural beauty of what God has created and clear the mind of the things in the world. Great idea!

Something else that has caused me great concern is how people can walk past you, only a few feet away, and not see you.

I enjoy acknowledging people as I pass by them going into stores. I like to smile at them and tell them hello. But people are becoming more and more reclusive. They duck their heads and rush by hoping you don't notice them. They seem sad and almost afraid.

I asked God how can this be. How can we not see each other when we are that close?

Maybe we have lost peripheral vision by staring at our computer or cell phone so much. By texting we can also cut down the hassle of getting emotionally involved with anyone. Texting has become a means of stating what you have to say in as few words as possible, even using initials, to talk to someone without feeling anything. Just words on a screen that you read and respond to. No feelings. No emotions, just dry matter-of-fact conversations.

Next time you receive a text try hearing it. Your mind will say, "hear what?' The answer will come back void and it will be a very profound feeling. (You have no balance?)

Does a repetitive use of one sense, without using every aspect of it, cause a malfunction?

Did God give us the ability to use each sense in many ways?

Do parts of our bodies become lazy when we don't use them? Of course we know the answer to this because we have learned the importance of exercise. "Use it or lose it." An old motto we have heard many times in our lives.

Peripheral vision is important in driving, and I think many wrecks are caused by not seeing the complete picture. Not only do we not use our peripheral vision, but we refuse to turn our head from one side to the other.

Does Society throw things at us so fast that we don't take time to critique them? Even if this is true what we did see, no matter how slight, is stored in our minds. (Memory banks.) When things are stored in our minds without any means of use it becomes like spam in a computer. It's there but has no practical use, just taking up space.

So what can we do about it?

First, be aware of what you watch. Be particular about what you store in your mind. The best thing is to never see it. We think because we change the channel when something bad comes on the TV that we have stopped the evil from entering our minds.

We have stopped any further evil from entering, but the part we did see is still there and will pop back up like spam when it's least expected. For instance, a commercial may come on that shows zombies and you see them and turn the channel, but late at night you may be awakened by a bad dream with zombies in it. You think, *"where did that come from?"*

Your mind stores everything your senses do. Your eyes saw the zombie before you turned the channel. If you had never seen the zombie, your mind would not have been able to recall it. It's that simple. Be careful what you do with your senses; remember everything is stored in your mind.

We are destroying the earth by doing too much, too quickly to it, without always protecting it in the process. Could we be doing this to our minds?

I have heard people say that it's okay for them to watch a violent or evil movie because they know it's not real and they can push it out of their minds when it is over. Doesn't affect them a bit. They know God and He will protect them. (Really?)

A person's mind can handle only so much evil. Over a period of time it causes our emotions to over load and shut down our senses. Without our senses our minds do not function. So could the mind be used to a much greater extent if we filled it with as much good as possible? Shouldn't we keep it in tune with God, so our emotions deal only with positive reactions from our senses?

I do believe our mind is not used to its capacity, but I think our emotions are being put on overload by the technologies of this world.

Could not seeing others as we pass by also be because we are so self- absorbed that nothing or no one matters to us? All we can think about is what we are doing. One foot in front of the other and let nothing get in the way.

When we pass someone nearly shoulder to shoulder and never see them, are we using our sense of sight as God had intended?

I started coming out of my depression when God told me to hold my head up and notice people around me. At first I was a little shocked, because I hadn't realized I had stopped.

When you sink into a depression you start isolating yourself from everything and everyone. In the process you slowly shut down your senses. Over a period of time you find it hard to relate to anything.

I think we start this because we want to shut

down our emotions. We don't want to experience hurt or pain anymore. We can't handle the drama of life so we stop connecting with the world. Then one day, we wake up in a dark hole of despair. We don't know how we got there and have no concept of how to get out.

Many people don't want out. They have accepted their gloom and find it easier than trying to survive the hardships of this world. Their isolation becomes their safety. They are free of emotional conflicts, not realizing they are shutting down their lives by shutting down the five things that keeps our minds functioning properly. When you shut down your senses you are no longer able to connect with God, so your sixth sense is even further removed than the other five.

The process of shutting down is slow at first and your connection with God becomes your life line as a Christian. You'll reach out and grasp anything you can to keep from sinking into despair. You start seeking advice from anyone you can. This in turn may cause an overload. Too much advice without a balance of your senses may cause anxiety.

You'll get an emotional overload that will make you feel like you are doing a juggling act. You juggle the advice one by one in a circle finding yourself afraid if you drop one, they will all fall and you will have to start over. Panic takes over and all you can think about is not dropping anything. You start grasping for straws. Anything that will give you some relief.

Anxiety adds to the depression because the thought of starting over brings fear into the mix of things. Fear is the root of anger and soon you become a basket case and you feel you are on an emotional roller coaster.

You don't want any more advise because you already have more than you can handle.You just want to stop but you can't for fear of losing your mind completely. So you keep holding on even if it isn't helping.

When you do drop it (juggling act) and you will, you may just look down and sadly say, *"What is the use of trying?"* Or *"I can't do this anymore."* This is the dark hole of despair. You give up.

When God made me aware of my sense of sight and that I had shut people out, I first asked Him to forgive me.

I started praying every day for God to make me aware of the people around me. Help me to see them as He did, and love them as He did.

I not only started seeing them, but I also began to listen to what they had to say. A whole new world was opened up to me and my mind began to clear. Because I was using my mind more, everything started making sense and I felt useful again.

People have some great stories. Try listening and truly enjoying them. It not only brings you joy, but it makes them happy as well. The connection you feel will be phenomenal.

There are a lot of good people in this world and God wants us to share our experiences with them. We are to be encouragers instead of discouragers.

Take time to listen and see how many doors

will open for you. You will expand your horizons.

When I added listening to my restricted little world I lived in, I started opening windows to the darkness I was in. I began to see a way out. I suddenly had hope.

That made me want to know more about my senses and what they contributed to my life. The more I studied the senses the more I knew I had the power to control what I stored in my mind. With that knowledge, God was able to teach me to use my senses properly and in line with Him. I started coming out of the depression.

Since the brain tumor I have had to take a prescription that causes depression. With the knowledge God has given me of my senses, I am able to combat that depression when it starts. I know how to get into the presence of God, and He guides me through everything that comes along.

One of my favorite ways to connect with God is when it rains. I find complete peace, because all my senses are used in a balance (Unity)

When it rains, you <u>hear</u> it. You <u>see</u> it and all the beauty it intensifies. The trees are greener, flowers brighter and everything looks cleaner. I can go touch it, but even if I don't, I know in my mind what it feels like because I have <u>touched</u> it before. I can taste it, or recall how it <u>tastes</u>. The crisp, fresh <u>smell</u> combines my senses with God, and I just bask in His creation and presence.

When you meditate upon God and learn to be in His complete presence through your senses, He will recharge you and dump the spam in your mind (the thoughts you don't need) just as you do with your computer when you dump the cookies.

By the way it is impossible to remain spam free in your mind because of the way the world is today. There is just too much information coming in and you can't shuffle through it and discard it fast enough. That is why meditating upon God is your only means of clearing the negative in your mind.

Going through life without truly seeing it is such a tragedy. God designed us in His image and He wants us to enjoy every part of it. Becoming too busy or just simply refusing to take time to see what He has created is the one of the worst ways we can abuse ourselves.

Not seeing the beauty in life and only acknowledging the tragedies will soon shut down the brain. You will begin to live life through your emotions and dread getting up in the morning. This will soon lead to fear and anxiety. We cannot function without the positive of God's presence.

God did not design us to be self-sufficient. We were always meant to be dependent upon Him. If we aren't dependent on Him then we are lost without direction, and our sight becomes blurred by the bad decisions we make. The worse our decisions become, the more we lead ourselves into darkness. God does not leave us. We leave Him by the wrong choices we make.

Do yourself a favor and start using your sight

to enjoy this great world God has created. There is so much beauty in life and unless you choose to see it, you won't.

Next time you're stuck in traffic, instead of becoming angry, look around you and see the sun and how it reflects off the trees giving it a greener hue. Notice the grass and the flowers along the highway. Admire the buildings and how unique their designs are and appreciate the work that was put into them. Enjoy the landscaping around them. Practice seeing positive instead of negative.

Being angry because of the delay of the traffic jam will not make the cars move any faster. I have learned to take delays in life as a free moment to rest, and connect with God.

Choosing to see the positive instead of the negative will put you in a far better mood when you finally get to your destination. It will also make the person you went to see happier.

Happy people are seldom ignored or rejected. Happiness from others is simply absorbed and admired.

Negative produces negative. People tend to retaliate the same way to mean behavior, or rudeness.

Along with free will to choose how we use our senses, God gave us the desire to learn. Although we learn from other senses, we seem to comprehend better from what we see. Maybe that is why we are such a visual society.

We can hear instructions on how to do things but when someone shows us how to do it as well, we learn faster and can remember it better. The vision of seeing it done brings it more to life and stores a vivid picture in our memory banks (Brains).

When you say the word "dog" to a group of people, everyone in that room will see a different dog in their minds. When you show a picture of a dog, everyone sees the same dog. Sight makes things more exact.

When we have children, we become aware of many of our faults, because they have such a desire to learn, they mimic many of the things we do. They try to talk, walk and sit the way we do and are very pleased with themselves when they succeed. It becomes very important to us to be a good example. "Monkey see, Monkey do," becomes more than a cliché when you become a parent.

CHAPTER FIVE

Hearing

My sheep listen to my voice; I know them, and they follow me.

John 10:27

*H*earing is the one sense that we have a tendency to shut down the most. We do this for many reasons. Sometimes out of self-preservation, other times from just free will, because we can. We just simply choose not to listen.

But before we get into that let's see how the Internet describes our sense of hearing: *Our ears, which help us hear, are made of two separate parts; the outer ear and the inner ear. The outer ear is the part that others see. It works like a cup to catch sound as it travels past our heads. This part is made of cartilage and skin. From here, sound travels to the tympanic membrane and then into the inner ear by the three smallest bones in your body. The inner ear is also called the cochlea. It is a spiral shaped tube which translates vibrations into sound and sends that message to the brain through the auditory nerve. The brain uses the sounds from both the left and the right ear to determine distance and direction of sounds.*

Our lives are animated by our hearing. Moving leaves on a tree have depth when we hear the sound of the wind. Birds singing bring a garden to life. Streets come to life when you hear the roar of the cars' engines, wheels turning and horns blowing. Towns come to life when people walk the streets. A smiling child touches our hearts when we hear their laughter. Peoples' words mean more to us when we hear the tone of their voices.

The world is full of noises, and the mind hears even when we are not trying to listen. The only time we don't hear is when we are sound asleep, but even then, sounds can wake us.

We have become so accustomed to noise that our minds don't register half of what we hear. We take it for granted and don't realize how important it is to our lives, unless for some reason, we lose it.

Life without hearing is living without emotions and no verbal direction. You are reliant on your sight to lead you as you go and will never hear the alarm when danger is near. You are dependent on what you see in front of you.

People who are deaf learn to use their other senses in more precise measures. Touch connects them to others. They rely on other peoples' reactions to guide them forward. Through sight they learn to read lips. Taste becomes a recognition of what they are eating and smell becomes an indicator of what they have eaten in the past. Smell can also be an indicator of danger. Unlike us, the deaf never take their senses for granted. Their senses control their lives because they depend on them to understand the world around them.

Amazing how such an intricate gift can be abused so badly and not used to its potential. Especially in this day and time.

Many times we shut down our hearing by telling our minds not to listen; literally tuning people out. We simply refuse to respond to the sound that is coming in. Some people call this selective hearing. I think this is dangerous to our minds because if we do this too much, it can become a normal response.

When I was a young adult, I was forced to be around a person that constantly told me what to do, when to do it, and how to do it. I started tuning her out. To my amazement one day, I found myself unable to hear a close friend of mine talking to me. I could see her mouth moving, but no sound was coming out.

Panic stricken, I strained to hear what she was saying. It took tremendous concentration, until finally I started hearing the words.

I learned it was dangerous to tune others out, and I have never intentionally tried to do so since. Be careful not to shut people out completely. Shutting people down by not listening to them does not protect you from getting hurt emotionally. It does however impair your ability to hear.

Learn to protect yourself from verbally abusive

people. Rely on the Holy Spirit to help you with people who won't help themselves, or who like to hurt others.

People who strike out at others are usually going through something and don't know how to deal with it. Lashing out becomes a defense mechanism for them. A means of holding you out at arms' length, or pushing you away.

Some people just like to complain. They seem to never be happy with anything. Maybe they just like to hear their own voices. I've never understood what makes them go on and on about nothing worth talking about. Perhaps they are in such misery, they must voice every miserable minute of their existence.

It takes patience and love to be around a contentious person. It is very hard to listen to them and have compassion, because nothing seems to make them happy. The Bible says in Proverbs 21:9: *It is better to live in the corner of the roof than share a house with a contentious woman.*

Men can be contentious, too and some verbally abusive. If you live with this and have done so for very long, you will probably need professional help. Verbal abuse is not just hard to listen to, it is mentally destructive.

The information I am giving in this book is about knowing your senses and learning to have positive responses in your everyday life.

Refusing to let people hurt you emotionally will make you stronger. Don't let what they say to you, get to you. Remember the old saying, *"Sticks and stones may break my bones, but words will never hurt me."*

I know people will argue this point and I do realize words hurt but what this phrase means is, words can only hurt you as much as you let them, but if someone throws a stone at you, there is nothing you can do to keep it from hurting. You have control over words and how they affect you, but you don't have control over sticks and stones. You get no choice in the size or intensity of what is hurled at you.

Being too sensitive can hurt you worse than what people say. Many times, people say things without knowing it hurts you. The art of not getting hurt when people say harmful things to you is hard at first. You have to realize it's not about 'me', you see past the emotional pain and start finding ways to help them. God doesn't intend for us to help others and be destroyed in the process. He'll give us all the tools we need to help others from the Fruits of His Spirit.

It takes a very strong Christian to help people who won't help themselves.

Society today is full of people who have mastered the art of getting as much from you as possible. They manipulate you with words that will touch your heart, and you find yourself giving them anything they want.

If this happens very often, over a period of time, you will start a spiral effect of shutting down and start avoiding people. We no longer want to get our emotions stomped on and we refuse to feel anything. We simply get tired of getting hurt. But when we shut down our emotions we shut down our brains where everything is stored. Depression sets in and everything we know and are is useless. It's like having a computer that's not plugged in; it's full of information but no way to receive it.

Simply walk away from someone you find impossible to help. Leave before they destroy you. This is known as tough love. It is more harmful to enable someone than to leave them. If you stay, you will be their crutch the rest of their life. There is never an end to their needs.

On the other hand, we can abuse ourselves by listening to things or shows that put us in an emotional overload.

Watching and listening to programs or music that causes us anxiety is not a good choice.

Getting too much, too fast thrown at us can cause us to shut down as well. We must have time to process what goes into our memory banks (Brains).

If we don't take time to evaluate the good from the bad, we will become an emotional basket case, unable to handle anything in life.

Television today is full of reality, drama, danger, violence and filth. All are designed to get us emotionally hooked. They want us to keep watching their programs so they use every technique they can to entice us. They are driven by ratings and we get sucked in.

Learn to filter what you watch and keep your emotions in check. Protect your mind.

Tragedies on television can cause post-partum

depression, if you have overcome similar disasters in your own life.

Reality shows have become a big trend in today's society, but be careful. Too much reality can cause an emotional overload as well. Be particular about what you allow to go into your mind. The old saying, "That things go in one ear and out the other" is not true.

Sensitive people need to be more protective of what they allow to go into the mind through their sight and hearing. Too much negative will put you on an emotional roller coaster. You'll have a hard time dealing with anything and never be able to understand why.

I was married for thirty years to a man who was a habitual liar. I did not believe in divorce, so I stuck it out much longer than I should have. I finally divorced him and a year later he died. It was a long, hard, and difficult marriage. I lived on an emotional roller coaster from beginning to end.

A few weeks after we were married, I found out that he slept with his best friend's wife the night before our wedding.

She starting working at the same restaurant I did about a month after our wedding. One day she came to me and told me everything about their trans-gression, including the fact that she was pregnant. Tough way to start a marriage.

My husband was in the Army and six months into our marriage we received orders to go to Germany. I finished high school and when he came back on leave he took me to Germany. I was a little farm girl; had never been out of Oklahoma very much.

After several months, his mother notified his commander and said that he and I were not legally married. When she took him and his sister and left her first husband, the divorce decree stated that she could never change her son's last name. She married another man and gave Lonnie (her son and my husband) the man's last name anyway. But it was never done legally. Because we had married using her second husband's name, our marriage was null and void.

It took well over a year to legally change his name to Northcliff. My oldest son was born a Northcliff and I was still a McCauley in the military hospital. It was a long drawn out affair.

My husband was an abused child and he learned to lie to keep from being beaten.

We went through so many situations and I learned to find solutions to the problems.

I became a problem solver because there was always a problem. God taught me so much and brought me through more than I care to talk about.

Because of my past I find it hard to date. Everyone wants to talk about their past. I can't. I made it through that time with God's help and I shouldn't have to relive it.

When the men talk about their past and the things that happened to them, I begin to get flash backs of my past.

I tell the guys to never tell me something bad someone has said about them because I look for the good in people. I say, "If you don't tell me, I may never see it, but if you tell me, I will never forget it."

Bad things in our past are just that, in the past. If you have asked God to forgive you, you require no other validation from anyone else. You just need to forgive yourself.

Most people can't handle their own mistakes, they certainly can't handle yours.

We ask way too much of others and then we are hurt when they let us down.

Only God knows how to restore us. Learn to listen to the Holy Spirit and allow Him to guide you in your life's journey. (The six senses.)

Another problem in today's society is: if it's not about them, they don't bother to listen. If the first few sentences don't mention their name or the conversation doesn't concern them, they leave.

When everything is about me, me, me, your entire life will be like living on a teeter-totter; up, down, up, down. You become so self-absorbed that nothing in life satisfies you. You become so wrapped up in yourself that people find it hard to be around you. You have no friends and loneliness begins to overwhelm you. Loneliness for very long will soon lead to depression.

God didn't design us to only think of ourselves. If we only think of ourselves, we are going to be very disappointed in life because the world does not revolve around us. Nothing will fulfill us in life; we'll feel unappreciated and unloved. It will become a very lonely existence. Anger will be a big part of our world because others won't see how truly wonderful we are. We become a legend in our own minds. Narcissism will control.

Life is about connecting to God and receiving the Fruits of His spirit, and sharing them with others. People truly make you happy when you share with them instead of taking from them.

Learn to listen to people. Friendships will have more depth when you listen to what others have to say. Share life with them by listening to memories from their past. People have some wonderful stories to tell.

CHAPTER SIX

Sixth Sense

For God so loved the world that He gave His only begotten Son, that whosoever believeth in him should not perish, but have everlasting life. (17) For God sent not His son into the world to condemn the world, but that the world through Him might be saved.

John 3: 16 - 17

*N*ow that we have talked about the five senses: <u>touch</u>, <u>taste</u>, <u>smell</u>, <u>hearing</u>, and <u>sight</u>, I want to introducc you to thc <u>sixth sense</u>. Many think the sixth sense is intuition, but I believe it is God. Before you accept the plan of salvation, there are times when you are warned when something is going to happen, because God is always with you, wanting to care for you.

If you haven't accepted Jesus Christ in your life, then this is the perfect opportunity for you do so. All you have to do is believe that Jesus Christ died for your sins and accept Him as your savior; then ask Him to come into your heart.

When you accept God's Son as your personal Savior, the Holy Spirit can enter you and become your guide throughout the rest of your life.

God loved us so much that He wanted to break the curse of death, the devil's power over us that Adam and Eve received from eating of the 'Tree of Knowledge.' They were cast out of the Garden of Eden and could no longer eat of the 'Tree of Life.'

When Jesus shed His blood it was not only His blood that ran from His body but also God's. God's blood sanctified us and gave us life eternal. Without God's Son we could not have defeated death. That is why it is so important to believe that God sent His Son to die for our sins, and why it is important to believe that this could only have been done through Jesus Christ, His Son. A blood descendant of the All Mighty God.

After Jesus' death and resurrection, He could no longer be with us in human form so He sent the Holy Spirit to live within us, to be our comforter, guide and teacher. Through the Holy Spirit we can receive the Fruits of the Spirit, which is God's essence.

If you accepted Christ into your life you are now able to experience the entirety of God. The Fruits of the Spirit are love, joy, peace, longsuffering, gentleness, goodness, faith, meekness and temperance. Without the Fruits of the Spirit, you will never have contentment in life, no matter how positive you try to be.

Once you become a believer in Christ, the attributes of God are at your fingertips. I want to show you how to have positive emotional responses through the Fruits of the Spirit. You no longer feel out of control because the gifts and blessings of God come to you when you listen to the Holy Spirit and let Him guide you through the trials of life.

The Fruits of the Spirit are your emotional responses to your senses. When you allow God's emotional responses in your life, your mind stores it in your memory bank as positive. When you repetitively have Godly responses to situations in your life, the mind will be filled with God and nothing the devil does can detour you.

On the left, I will list the Fruits of the Spirit and across from it I will list the fruits of the Devil so that you can see how to counteract the negative responses.

GOD	Devil
• Love	Hate
• Joy	Anger
• Peace	Turmoil
• Longsuffering, (Tolerance)	Impatience
• Gentleness	Hardness
• Faith	Doubt
• Meekness	Brash, Vain
• Temperance	Hostility

Any emotional response you can come up with can be derived from these words. The more you learn to have good positive responses, the more

God rewards you with His presence. The only way we can become more like God is to practice memory responses that connect us to Him.

To help you understand how to have Godly responses instead of the Devil's, I'm going to break it down for you in examples.

If you become angry with someone during a conversation, before you react, try to figure out what is causing you to be mad. Is it what they are saying, or your old emotional responses causing you to feel such a reaction? You need to get to the root of your response before you can respond well to others.

Many times, when a person begins to raise his/her voice in a conversation, you will automatically become defensive. Especially if you have been yelled at quite a bit in your lifetime. You may respond in the same manner as you have in the past even if someone hasn't said anything to hurt you. Just the fact that someone raised his/her voice put you on the defense. The emotional response you have had in the past will cause you to retaliate. You may strike out at the first person by yelling back, which will escalate into a huge fight that leaves you both wondering what happened.

If what someone says doesn't really affect you other than raising his/her voice, put yourself in check and tell yourself, this is not about me. When you do this, you are more apt to be able to help that person.

Many times we miss an opportunity to help someone else because we let our past reactions get in the way. The more we realize life is not only about ourselves, the more we are able to do God's work by helping others.

Often times we are unable to help others because we have a tremendous fear of being hurt. Once we have been hurt by someone we will go to great lengths to protect ourselves from any further pain.

If you find yourself reacting to someone from the fruits of the Devil, before you voice your opinion look at the opposite of what you are feeling and rely on the Holy Spirit. If you are angry, the Holy Spirit will lead you to God's Fruit, which is temperance. If you're feeling impatient, look to tolerance, etc. Be aware of the Fruits of the Spirit and implement them in your life at all times. The more you connect with people in this manner, the more you connect to God. You also introduce them to God through your reactions. People who do not know God, do not know Godly responses to anything in their lives.

I know it is not always easy to respond to some people through the Fruits of the Spirit, but the more you practice them, the more they are stored in your mind as a positive memory response. Soon it will become automatic.

The more we use the Fruits of God's Spirit in our life the more we become like God. Self is no longer the controlling factor in our decisions; love is.

You cannot receive the Fruits of the Spirit by hoarding them. Just like love, you never receive it until you give it. God rewards us with His Fruits when we practice His attributes on others.

If you are around someone who causes you to feel hate, ask yourself why you hate that person.

What is causing that memory response? Have they done something to you in the past, or do you simply find them repulsive? If this is the case, stop noticing all the bad characteristics of that person, and try to see the good in them. Even the most obnoxious people have something good about them. Ask the Holy Spirit for guidance. The only way to counteract a hate response is to find something to love about that person.

The more you see the good in others, the more God rewards you with His Love.

My prayer everyday includes asking God to make me more aware of the people around me; to see them through His eyes, so I can love them as He does.

If someone worries excessively, he/she is in great turmoil. Introduce them to God's peace. The peace that surpasses all understanding.

If you are in turmoil, go to God and pray for His peace. Peace in this world can come only from God. Turn it over to God completely if you are unable to handle it yourself. God doesn't mind taking charge, but He won't do it unless you ask Him to. Unlike the devil, God will not force Himself on you. He takes charge of a situation only when you give it to Him. You will be astonished at the speed and accuracy of the results you get. God's plan is so much better than ours.

Before I made a war room to pray in, I prayed at the front side of my bed. I would tell people where I prayed and that I kept my tennis shoes at the foot of the bed, because when I turned everything over to God, I'd have to run to keep up.

It's amazing how fast God can work when we get out of His way and just do what He tells us to do.

If you are angry and unhappy you need to find some joy in your life. Don't dwell on the bad things that happen; look around and appreciate all the good you have. You may not have as much as some do, but what you have is from the Lord and He alone can give you the joy you need.

Just enjoying a beautiful day with all He has created is enough to make me happy.

If people are hard-hearted or harsh, treat them with kindness. Don't respond negatively. It is hard to be mean to a person smiling at you. Be gentle with them. They have so much hurt inside of them that it flows out of their mouth like a fountain. They have no faith and their world is filled with constant doubt. Being abrasive back to them just makes them angry. Do not try to fight back with them. They are always ready for a fight and they will win because they've had a lot more practice.

In my early career as a hairstylist I was the manager of a popular chain of hair salons. As manager I had to deal with all complaints. That's when I received a hard lesson on not fighting back.

People who are angry are ready for the fight. They have been practicing in their mind for hours, even days. One negative word out of my mouth and they pounced. They'd call me names, attack my professionalism and come at me any way they could.

I learned to look past the name calling and try to just hear what the problem was.

It didn't matter what they called me; they didn't know anything about me. What they did know was they wanted their money back, and they were going to do whatever it took to get it. I had to look past that and focus on the problem.

Let the Holy Spirit guide you. Whenever your response is on the devil's side, look across the list and see what you need to pray and tap into. Over a period of time you will have many more positive responses than negative. I wish I could tell you you'll never have another negative response, but I can't, because as long as the devil is here with us on earth, he will never stop trying to deceive us.

Instead of shutting down our mind by not responding to the devil, tap into the source (God) that can give us everything we need, and then some.

CHAPTER SEVEN

Talking Is Not A Sense

*"For in many things we offend all. If any man of-
fend not in word, the same is a perfect man, and
is able to bridle the whole body."*

James 3: 2 KJV

$\mathcal{M}$any people are under the misconception that talking is one of the five senses. Talking is a means of communicating but it is not one of our senses that God gave us to connect with Him and others. Talking is like our arms, legs, hands, feet, it is a body function. Talking is a verbal reaction to our senses. It is a loud response to what we have stored in our memory. Just like a printer that is connected to a computer and can copy anything we have stored on the hard drive (memory bank) when we instruct it to. Except sometimes we have a verbal response without instructions from our brain because we have not tried to restrict the tongue by thinking before we speak. This is where common sense comes in. Wikipedia says common sense is: *A basic ability to perceive, understand, and judge things, which is shared by nearly all people, and can be reasonably expected of nearly all people without any need to debate.*

Actually you get common sense from the consequences of bad reactions to your senses and from learning to respond in a positive way. If you never try to learn from your mistakes you will never learn what is good and what is bad. Unfortunately, your tongue will be the proof of your inability, it will hurt others as well as yourself. That is why it is so important to understand your five senses and to be careful how you use them. They are what stores memories in your mind. Your tongue will tell on you. You really should think before you speak.

One day my oldest son came home from high school and as he walked through the door I said to him, "Make sure you clean your room."

"I don't have to; I like it the way it is," he told me somewhat defiantly.

"Don't talk to me that way!" I warned him.

I was astounded when he replied, "My teacher in my psychology class said I have the right to say anything I want to. We all have freedom of speech and what I have to say is important."

"Really, she says it's okay to disobey your parents?" I exclaimed.

"She says we all have a right to our opinion and we should never be afraid to speak out," he said, defiantly.

"Even if it hurts someone's feelings?" I asked.

"Well you say I should always tell the truth," he declared boldly.

"Not if it hurts people's feelings." I insisted.

"Well make up your mind, should I tell the truth or not?" he demanded.

"Only if they ask you what you think. The truth sometimes hurts." I said trying to make him understand that you shouldn't tell people everything you perceive about them unless they ask you for your opinion. That way they are prepared for your opinion.

"Well, make up your mind, should I tell the truth or not?" he said turning away from me and walking down the hall to his room.

I stood there in shock, staring at his back as he walked away, thinking, *'What about the golden rule? Do unto others as you would have them do unto you.'* I shook my head wondering what this kind of teaching was going to do to our world.

Now, twenty some years later the new generation is full of opinions, with everyone talking and no one listening. Bullying in schools and on the Internet, with children thinking they have the right to say anything and do anything without being held accountable for it. What's worse it is rubbing off onto all of us. Everyone is talking and no one wants to listen. We are critical of others and we think we have the right to tell everyone what is wrong with them. No wonder we are losing our minds!

Some people are so busy talking they never have time to think. Sometimes you may secretly wish for an off button. The only way to get them to stop is to say or do something that causes them to think. You cannot think and talk at the same time.

To get someone to stop talking they have to listen. That is why hearing is one of the five senses. To get them to listen you have to talk about something that interests them. In most cases, that would be something about themselves. They are so self-absorbed that the only thing they comprehend is things that are about them.

Have you ever walked up to a table with seven or eight people seated around it and everyone is talking? The worst part about it is that everyone is talking about something different? Not one person is listening. The reason for this is that when the first person started a conversation the person next to them was 'set off' by a trigger word that brought out a memory of something that was stored in their mind, then the person beside them gets a trigger word and it continues all around the table.

What is a trigger word? Our minds are just like a computer. When you want to look up something on the Internet and you don't know what it is called exactly, you put a word into Google that relates to what you want to look up. The search engine will pull up several things related to what you are searching for. That is called a trigger word. It pulls up things that are used the most by the average person first, but sometimes it pulls up subjects that have nothing to do with what you want. You have to weed through them to find what you want, or you may have to put in another trigger word. Sometimes you have to put in more of an explanation.

We have become such a society of talkers and no one is listening. Worse than that we have become so self-absorbed that trigger words bring up our own memories and we talk about ourselves instead of listening to others. Listening is a dying art. We are neglecting one of our important senses, hearing. Then we sit around wondering why we are going deaf. God designed our body to be used. We don't lose our senses by too much use, we lose them by not using them at all. But we must have a balance of our senses.

Let me give you an example of what happens at a table when no one is listening and everyone is talking. There are eight people seated at a table with a full plate in front of each of them. No one is talking, then someone says, "These green beans are really good. What do you think they put in them that makes them taste so good?" The lady next to the person says, "My husband hated green beans. He never let me make them and I just loved them........" She's off on a conversation about her husband. Another person says, "I think it's onions. They are chopped so small you can hardly see them........." She's off talking about how to chop onions. The person next to them says, "I hate onions, we lived on a farm when I was young and my mother put onions in everything........." The next person says I was raised on a farm and my Dad worked me from sun up to sun down. The only break I got was when I went to school. But as soon as I got home, mother made sure I got busy with......" The person beside them says, "I don't care what they put in it, I can't take my eyes off this dessert. I can't wait to taste it. Doesn't it look fabulous.........." The person beside them says, "I didn't get dessert, I'm a diabetic and my doctor says I can't have too many sweets.........." The person next to them says, "I went to the doctor last week and he says my heart is off rhythm........."

Did you catch the trigger words? This is how people are having conversations these days. Believe me, the tongue is one muscle that we don't need to exercise. We would see each other much differently if we suddenly lost the power to use it. We would be forced to use our five senses which would connect us with people more effectively with lasting results. James 3:2: *For in many things we offend all. If any man offend not in word, the same is a perfect man, and able also to bridle the whole body.*

James 3:8: *But the tongue can no man tame; it is an unruly evil, full of deadly poison.*

Negativity is another reason our minds are shutting down. God expects us to build each other up and work together in harmony and unity. When you say something negative to other people you are tearing them down, destroying their self-esteem. Too much negativity can cause a person to shut down their mind completely because they cannot handle the abuse. They shut it out in order to survive. When we don't have a Godly balance of all our senses we start shutting them down one at a time. This causes an overload on the senses that ARE being used.

James 3:18 KJV says, *The fruit of righteous-ness is sown in peace of them that make peace.* God gives us love, joy, peace, patience, kindness, goodness, faithfulness, gentleness, and self-control. Ask yourself these questions: Are attributes of God coming out of my mouth? Am I using my tongue just to be able to hear myself talk? Do I find beauty in everyone as God does in me? Do I see the uniqueness of everyone as God does in me? Do I love others as I want them to love me? Do their hurts and concerns bother me? Do I show as much kindness to others as I want them to show me? Am I nice to others first or do they have to first show kindness to me?

James 1:23,24 KJV says, *For if any man be a hearer of the word, and not a doer, he is like unto a man beholding his natural face in a glass: (24) For he beholdeth himself; and goeth his way, and straightway forgetteth what manner of man he was.* So in other words, if you don't do what the Bible instructs you to do it is like looking in the mirror at yourself and, when you walk away, you forget what you looked like.

I could fill a book on talking and how we misuse it. I want you to understand the importance of using your senses in balance with God. Our relationship with God and others depends on this balance. When we have a complete balance of our senses through the Holy Spirit, we have a complete understanding of God. Our life is filled with such joy it overflows onto everyone around us. 1 John 4:4b: *Greater is He that is in you, than he that is in the world.*

If you have negativity coming out of your mouth, **you do not have clarity from God**. You may need more information or more instruction. You may just need to get with God and pray, but there is nothing about God that is negative. Negative is a 'what if,' God has nothing to do with 'what if's,' because He is a Sovereign God. He knows everything from beginning to end. When we say 'what if' we are actually leaving God out and trying to find solutions on our own.

'What ifs' will take control of our thinking process and we will lose our ability to enjoy life, because we have opened ourselves up the temptations of the devil. We start second guessing God and start making scenarios that will fall in line with what we want to happen.

We'll find ourselves failing at everything we do because nothing comes out as we had planned. People around us become the problems to our success and we strike out at anyone that gets in our way. We find fault in everyone and we start trying to perfect them by criticizing their every move.

We start taking out our frustrations on the people closest to us and we never find any joy in our life because the people we should be loving and sharing things with have become our enemies and undermine everything we try to do.

We feel unloved, unappreciated and used when around people. We find it hard to receive love because in the back of our mind they are after something we have, or they will want us to do something we don't have any desire to do.

'What ifs' will cause you to lose the balance you have in your life.

CHAPTER EIGHT

Emotions

The preceding chapters have introduced you to your senses and how important they are to your mind. I have touched on some of the emotional responses we have to our senses, but in this chapter I want to explain in depth the importance of having good responses to our senses.

People are on an emotional overload these days. Everything hurts their feelings. I think a big part of that is because people aren't talking face to face. They're either emailing on a computer or texting on their phones. The phone has become everyone's life lock. They can't live without it. Some can't bear to set it down. They panic when they misplace it for even a moment.

Texting and emailing are so unfeeling. Simply words on a screen. The young have a universal language all their own, by putting letters together without spelling.

I had an email conversation with a guy once

from another state for an hour and a half one evening. Many times after typing something I would put LOL after it. At the end of the conversation he said, by the way what does LOL mean? I said, "Laugh out loud." He said, "Oh I thought you were saying 'lots of love.' I was thinking, man, those women in Oklahoma sure are loving people." LOL. I guess there can be some fun in texting, but it's not nearly as much fun as actually listening to people and truly laughing out loud.

We judge the things we do by the way it makes us feel. If it makes us feel good, we'll do it again. Where we go and what we do depends on what we are going to get out of it. No one thinks of doing things for others, simply because it would make that person happy. Their mentality is: don't have time to waste.

If someone hurts our feelings, makes us sad or miserable, we don't go around them. We don't face our feelings by talking and working them out, we just store bad responses on top of bad responses. We are afraid of getting hurt so we stay away from people, or we retaliate by striking out at everyone we see. Hurt them before they have a chance to hurt us.

The Bible says if we have anything against our brother we are to go to him and work it out. Ask for forgiveness if you are the one in the wrong. When we work out our problem with others it gets rid of bad responses in our memory banks. The hard feelings we once had will disappear if we allow them to. Working problems out with others will make you stronger emotionally. Your mind will have more positive memory responses.

God tells us to forgive our brother, if he asks for it. Not forgiving someone will eat away at your brain. It destroys any positive responses from that point on. You can't think of anything else.

I read a story once about a man walking in the town square. He stopped, leaned over and picked up a string and put it in his pocket. Shortly after that a man came running up to him with a police officer saying, "That's him. That's the man who found my wallet in the square. I saw him lean over, pick it up, and put it in his pocket."

The man said, "I didn't pick up a wallet." He reached in his pocket and pulled out the string and said, "I found this piece of string."

The officer arrested him and then later released him for lack of evidence.

The man was so angry that he carried that piece of string around with him everywhere he went and told the story of how he was wrongfully accused to anyone who would listen.

Many years later they found him dead, lying in a ditch. His old clothes where dirty and torn and he had nothing to his name, but when they opened his clinched hand they found an old piece of string.

Caring a grudge is harmful to you. Your mind can't think of anything but how you were falsely treated. There is no room in your mind for any other responses, because you don't allow it. You become an angry, bitter person, thinking the whole world is out to get you.

Our minds are so full of responses that we can just think of an emotional feeling such as being sad, and pull up unlimited incidents in our life that made us unhappy. It won't stop until we concentrate on another response, such as being happy. You can over-ride the negative response by concentrating on something positive. The time it takes to counter-act the negative will depend on how much you have allowed the negative to consume you. If you decide you don't want to stop the sadness, then you won't. Positive emotional thoughts bring positive results.

The most important thing you will learn in life is that everything is not about you. There is no way the world can make you happy. What you feel in-side is what will, or will not, make you happy. If you don't have God in your heart you will struggle your whole life with the "me syndrome." Nothing you do will ever satisfy you.

The "me Syndrome" can quickly spiral out of control when you take God out of the equation. The reason for this is 'me' is always looking for instant pleasure. Remember I talked earlier about how the devil gives you pleasure. (Fleeting.) The Lord gives you contentment. (Lasting.) Because pleasure is only for a moment we find ourselves looking for more and more things that will give us pleasure, thinking it will bring us happiness. Over a period of time this forms an addiction.

Instead of using your senses to have positive reactions, you start living your life through your emotions. As I said in the beginning of the book, emotions are the reactions to the responses of your senses. If you're not using your senses in a positive way, you are going to have an emotional response that repeats itself over and over again in a negative way. Which will soon cause you an emotional overload that triggers many negative responses, such as hate, loneliness, bitterness, anger and fear. These negative responses will leave you feeling, tired, unloved, unappreciated, overworked, and inadequate.

You may go to extremes and consider everyone around you inadequate. These extreme emotions will cause you to go into overdrive and strike out at people without any warning or control. I've heard the younger people call it a melt-down.

A melt-down can be an out of control yelling at someone with no filter on what you say, to uncontrollable crying.

You can control what you do with your senses, but you can't control your emotional responses if you don't have healthy positive reactions stored in your mind.

When you get into the extremes of these emotions you start concentrating on "me" too much out of self-preservation. It starts out as a way to control your emotions, but over a period of time it becomes a necessity to survive.

When this fails, which it will, you start trying to control everyone around you so you can have order. If your emotions get out of whack, you strike out at anything or anyone that messes up your order.

At this point you feel if you don't get order

you will self-destruct. You become impossible to live with because you want everything in your life to be perfect. You expect your children, husband/wife, relatives, co-workers and employees to be perfect, because if they are not, you will go into an emotional overload. Everything becomes chaotic. You feel like you are standing on the edge of a cliff and the least little nudge will push you over the side. Nothing anyone does or says makes your world right.

You wake up one day and say, "How did I get here? What has given me this feeling of failure. Why can't people see me for the great person I have become? I do everything right, or pretty close. Close enough to perfect as I possibly can. Why don't people appreciate me. I work hard. Surely this is all their fault. They can't see me as I truly am. I know what I'll do, I'll try a little harder and then if they don't see me as I truly am, I'll just tell them what I think of them. Point out their imperfections. See how they like that.

I'll give you a simple example of how we do things that can have a very negative effect on us.

You post a picture of yourself on social media; you get a hundred likes. Then you get someone that criticizes you so precisely that you have to look at the picture again to make sure you sent the right one. You suddenly forget about the hundred that liked it and start to see yourself as that person saw you. You become disgusted with yourself and think of ways you can improve your looks.

You change a few things about your appearance and post again. This time you get ninety-nine likes and two people who criticize you. You say, "What!"

"Okay, I'll do more," you angrily say out loud while looking at yourself in the mirror. So, you put more makeup on to cover some of the flaws they talk about and highlight other areas you feel are your best features. Thinking, *'surely, they will like this.'*

You post again. This time ninety-eight likes and three dislikes. Your emotions start going off the charts. *'This is getting crazy,'* you say to yourself as you start feeling overly criticized, unappreciated, unloved and completely rejected. Which in turn makes you respond with hate, anger, and complete fear.

You hate them for not liking you. You're angry because they don't even know you and you find yourself wanting to retaliate. Fear takes over and you're not sure why. You haven't done anything wrong. You just posted a picture you thought looked great. This is where rejection takes over and you start shutting down, or you retaliate. You say, *"I'll just tell them what I think about them."*

You call them names, talk about how insensitive they are, attack their character and may even call them ugly. (Even though you may not know what they look like.)

Bam! Fifty dislikes and others telling you, "That's telling them," and they start bashing the people that disliked you, too.

Suddenly your beautiful picture starts to make you feel like a horrible person. Even the ones who agreed with you, make you feel ugly and dirty.

What have you just done with your senses? You have taken just one sense, your sense of sight, and caused a ripple effect of responses and emotions that will be stored in your mind, that will resurface next time you think about posting again. If you don't learn from this experience and post again and again, you will develop a pattern of negative and hurtful responses that will soon begin to shut down the rest of your senses. You won't want to see, hear or touch anybody and you certainly won't want anyone to see, hear or touch you. You think you can protect yourself from any further pain, and you begin shutting down your emotions so you don't have to feel anything.

When you are rejected on social media, you begin to avoid people you actually come into contact with face to face. You begin to see yourself as the person that criticized you, and become afraid of everyone you see. As you walk by them, you duck your head and hope they don't see your flaws and think, *'I must not let them see me too closely, because I would just die if they looked at me with disgust or, heaven forbid, they might mention how ugly I look.'*

The devil loves to point out your flaws and wants you to dwell on the negative sides of your character. When he gets you to react to situations through your emotions, he knows you will do anything to gain control.

You begin using your senses in many negative ways, because you want to be in charge of your life.

When you sink into the 'me syndrome' you begin to think only you can solve your problems. You fight and struggle to stay in charge of every situation that comes along.

The more you fight to stay in control, the fewer positive reactions you have to your senses, because many times you are just grasping for anything that will bring you some sort of happiness.

Happiness becomes unattainable because you don't have the Holy Spirit guiding your responses to your senses. The more bad responses you store in your memory bank (mind), the more your negative responses repeat themselves and your emotions go off the chart.

When the devil gets you to react to situations through your emotions, he knows you will do any-thing to gain control even if it means shutting down your mind to have peace in your life. When isolating yourself from others doesn't bring you the peace you wanted, you climb into a hole of despair and you no longer use your senses to connect you to the world around you. You may even consider suicide. This is how the darkness of the world takes over your life.

When we learn about God and the Fruits of His Spirit, we see light overshadow the darkness. Love becomes a natural response and the Joy of the Lord starts controlling our emotions.

Getting back to posting on social media, you may be asking yourself, *'well if I knew God how would this situation have been different?'*

1. You may never have posted in the first place. When you truly know God, you have no desire to be seen for the sake of being seen. You know who you are and the Fruits of His Spirit bring you complete joy and satisfaction. The only reason you want to be seen is for them to see the Love of God that shines within you.

2. If you do post a picture, (which by the way is not a sin) you will not respond to any negative feedback. The Holy Spirit will guide you in a positive way and instruct you to respond with kindness, and appreciate their opinion.

The people in the world today are so opinionated they think they have the right to say anything they want to, without any concern for other's feelings.

When you know God, you understand Ephesians 4:29 KJV: *Do not let any unwholesome talk come out of your mouths, but only what is helpful for building others up according to their needs, that it may benefit those who listen.*

God wants us to build each other up and help each other when we are down. We will all have emotional situations in our lives but when we turn to God and help each other, He will give us the strength and understanding to get us over emotional responses that try to destroy us.

God intended for us to help each other and be strong together. In Ecclesiastes 4:12 KJV says: *And if one prevail against him, two shall withstand him; and a threefold cord is not quickly broken.*

When we try to go through life alone without the help of others and God, nothing in life has any meaning. Our purpose is wasted when we only think of ourselves and how life makes 'us' feel. When we only store our own opinions of ourselves, it comes back to us void, emotionally.

When we truly know God and learn to be in His presence, we can feel love, joy, peace, patience, kindness, goodness, faithfulness, gentleness and self-control all at one time. The emotional response you get from this is total and complete awe. (I like to tell people it is more than awesome. Awe-some is just some awe. When you are in God's presence you are in total and complete Awe.)

Once you have experienced God's Fruits, then you have a desire to share His Fruits with everyone you meet.

Self is no longer a controlling factor in your life, because sharing God's Fruits comes back to you and fills you even more. The more you give, the more you get back.

When you know God's love and truly fill it in your heart, you have a desire to share that love with others. 'Me' is no longer the important factor in your life and you have a desire to serve instead of being served.

The more you serve and share your life with others the more meaning you develop in your life. You no longer live on an emotional roller coaster and you get joy from seeing other people happy. Your life has more meaning and you lose that emotional feeling of failure. You suddenly have purpose and

God continually rewards you for helping others and loving them as He does.

Nothing about yourself is great unless you have God in your heart guiding you through life. Constantly trying to dig down deep within yourself to find that fabulous person inside of you will only cause you to turn yourself inside out, and soon you are so lost you can't find a way to make yourself right again.

Emotions are great when they are positive and come from God's Fruit, but when you have negative emotions you are allowing the devil the opening he needs to destroy your mind and life.

Do yourself a favor and stop worrying about 'me' so much and listen to the Holy Spirit, so God can guide your life and preserve your mind. The difference will be profound.

CHAPTER NINE

Exercise Your Senses

Now that you know your senses and the importance of them, I want to give you some suggestions on how to exercise them. Just as our bodies need to stay in shape to function properly, so do our minds.

Over the years we use our senses in so many different ways that we abuse our own mental capacities. We've used, abused and set them free.

The one thing we do not want to do is set them free. Your senses keep your mind alert, so what we need to do is sharpen our senses. This is something God has shown me recently and as I exercise my senses more I find I am becoming mentally healthier by the day. I'm laughing more and find humor in things I had been taking too seriously during depression.

The Bible says in Proverbs 17:22 (KJV): *"A merry heart doeth good like a medicine, but a broken spirit drieth the bone."*

Wow, that's pretty clear: If you refuse to laugh you will rot away to the bone. Who would have thought that by refusing to see the humor in life, we would destroy ourselves?

An old Yiddish proverb says, *"What soap is to the body, laughter is to the soul."* Everyone knows that laughter makes you feel good and puts you in high spirits, but did you also know that laughter actually causes physiological responses that protect the body from disease and help your vital organs to repair themselves?

A good laugh is a way to exercise the brain. Just as working out helps the muscles and blood flow to the brain, laughing can decrease blood pressure and stress hormones, improves sleep patterns and boost the immune system. A study by the John Hopkins Medical School showed that humor and laughter can also improve memory and sharpen mental performance.

Some simple suggestions that can help you to enjoy life more:

Don't take life too seriously. We all have problems in life and we are going to make mistakes, but we don't have to let them control us. Learn to laugh at your mishaps and you will find it easier to try new things, because you won't be so afraid of failure. You'll be more willing to try again. A mistake is not a disaster, it is a minor inconvenience. This also extends to other people. Don't be too hard on others. Expecting too much from others can stress you out as much as trying to be perfect yourself. A smile and a chuckle are much more effective than criticism.

Try to find humor in bad situations. There are many situations in life that make you sad and don't warrant laughter, but try to look at the irony of the problem. Laughing at bad situations lowers the stress level. It helps you to think more clearly and not become anxious. Worry and anxiety can increase the cortisol in your body that affects your blood pressure, blood sugar and heart rate.

Remind yourself of funny moments from the past. When you are extremely sad, try to think of something that made you happy. Conjure up a memory that brought you laughter. Don't dwell on the things that are sad. Don't give into sadness and anger. Reliving funny moments in your life causes the endorphins to kick in, which act as a natural pain killer that will bring you joy.

Surround yourself with people who enjoy laughing. Hang out with people who enjoy life and see the humor in everyday living. People who aren't afraid to laugh at themselves and don't mind if you laugh at them. They will lighten your mood and help you realize you don't have to be correct and perfect all the time.

Get a pet. Animals love you unconditionally and they have a great desire to make you happy. They love to play, and many things they do bring you joy and cause you to laugh. Studies have proven that animals can keep you from being lonely and help fight off depression. They can also lower your stress levels and protect you from heart disease.

Who would have thought laughter could do so

much to protect our bodies and minds?

At group gatherings, you will notice that the people at the tables that are silent are glancing at the tables where people are laughing and having fun. The yearning in their eyes says, *"I wish I was at that table."*

Some may come over to the table and say, "This seems like a fun table. What are you all laughing about?" Everyone looks up as they stop laughing and respond in unison, "I don't know." Then they look at each other and laugh again.

Everyone at the table is in a happy mood because someone started them laughing. After a while you see humor in everything, even those asking what is funny. It becomes a natural response to laugh. It doesn't take long for your mind to recall laughter when you have done it before repetitively.

Someone who never or very seldom laughs will not find anything you tell them funny. You can try and try to make them laugh but it is not a normal response for them.

If you very seldom laugh, try to think of something that you truly found laugh-out-loud funny at one time. You may have to concentrate to recall every detail but you will soon get there. Then do it repetitively until you get used to laughing. There is no shame in laughing. People love it. Even if your laugh is weird to you, people don't care. That can be funny too.

I was married to my husband for years before he laughed out loud. I asked him why he didn't and he said, "My laugh is weird and people used to make fun of me, so I quit it."

So what if people think it is weird. Laughing is fun no matter how you do it. When I was a teenager I used to practice laughing different ways. I could entertain myself for hours.

If you're afraid of people making fun of you, practice in front of a mirror and do funny expressions, or laughs. It's fun to see your facial expressions as well. I used to talk like Mae West in front of the mirror and found it even more hilarious because of the way I had to distort my face to match her actions. Fun stuff.

When I was overseas in Germany I worked in the office of an NCO Club. One day I was doing paper work and listening to the radio behind me that was turned down low. They were interviewing a man whose job was to go into public places and laugh to see how many people he could get to laugh. He started out slowly at first and then worked his way into a contagious laugh that you couldn't help but laugh with him. My boss came in while the man was escalating his laugh and sat down in a chair reading some papers. As the man proceeded, I began laughing. The harder he laughed, the harder I laughed.

My boss would read, look up at me, go back to reading as though he couldn't hear the man on the radio. Maybe he couldn't, but finally after observing me in this unusual manner, he put the paper down and said, "What the h--- is wrong with you?"

All I could do was point at the radio behind me and laugh. He stood up and walked out as if I was crazy.

When I finally stopped laughing I thought, *'What a fun job that would be.'*

Forty years later I can still laugh and recall how hilarious that man was. When you start exercising your senses to laugh, you will use your sight and hearing the most. The more you refresh your memory of laughter, the more you will recall things in your past that you found funny. Recalling memories is a must in exercising your senses.

Write down some of your stories you recall from the past, and put them in a box so you can read them on a bad, gloomy day. Keeping your mind in a positive, productive state will restore your memory. Negative thoughts will shut down your memory and you will regress.

<u>Taste</u>: A sense we do so automatically that we seldom recall what we have eaten hours later.

Or we multi-task while eating. Which, as I said earlier in the book, will confuse your memory responses. Whatever you were concentrating on the most will be what is stored in your mind.

To exercise taste, try this: eat one item on your plate at a time. Try to figure out what you like about it; texture, color, ingredient, flavor, how it looks. You might even like the way it smells the best. Let your mind recall memory responses of the past. Savor it; enjoy it. Give it your undivided attention.

I realize you don't have time to do this every

time you eat, but remember you are exercising. Give it an allotted time as you would physical exercise. Realize you are trying to build up your memory bank so that your mind will last longer. If this brings pleasure and you find it enjoyable, you will have stored a positive response in your brain that you will want to repeat. When you become comfortable with this, you will learn to dine instead of just cramming food into your mouth to fill a void. Remember God gave us our senses so we could enjoy every aspect of life. Being thankful for what you are eating will let you leave the table with a comforting feeling of approval from God.

I have a friend who hates meal time because her husband dislikes everything he eats. Whether she cooks it or they go out to eat, he complains about everything.

Years ago they came up with statistics claiming families that sat at the table and ate their meals together were closer.

Smell: Take time to actually smell food, cologne, flowers, people, buildings, etc. Everything has a distinct odor. Remember it is either a new memory or old memory. Smelling your food gives it a more enticing appeal and even makes it taste better.

I told my friend the other day that I love to go into Barnes and Noble, or any book store, because it has a special smell all its own. As I was telling her I tried to recall what it smelled like. I simply said, "It smells like knowledge." It always smells the same and I get an empowering feeling of being surrounded by an immense amount of intelligence.

Listening to someone talk who has an attractive perfume on makes you hang on every word. You don't have to be attracted to them, or lured in. You simply enjoy how they smell and you find the entire conversation enjoyable. You walk away with a positive, pleasant experience. Personally, if a man has on a nice cologne, I could listen to him as long as he wanted to talk.

My dad's favorite cologne was Old Spice. To this day when I smell it on a man. I instantly give him the same attributes as my father, thinking, *'That man must be a strong, quiet man with a lot of common sense.'* That may sound silly considering I don't know him, but my mind brings up the memory of a man that I did know. Walking past the man has brought to my mind a very happy memory.

Familiar smells will bring life back to your mundane world. The more you use your sense of smell the more memory experiences you will have. Certain smells put your mind in movie mode and you can visualize the past as clearly as when you were there the first time. Our senses working together in a balance will bring you a depth to life you would normally ignore.

"Take time to smell the roses," may be a cliché', but it brings life to still objects. It puts your mind in motion. We think the more we do, the more we get accomplished, the better our life will be. That depends on whether or not you enjoy what you're doing. If the entire day was filled with unpleasant experiences, no positive has been added to your memory.

When you enjoy everything you have done,

your mind stays in a positive motion, and you'll crave more. You'll never overload on positive responses, but the negative will pile up end on end and you'll feel drained and used up.

Multi-tasking: When we do too many things at one time it leaves our mind wondering what should be stored and what shouldn't. Many times it goes in as spam, just floating around taking up valuable space. I'd much rather have valuable information stored from my senses than something that pops up when you least expect it and you say to yourself, *'Where did that come from?"'* You rapidly shake your head and hope it goes away. It doesn't.

The more you use your sense of smell the more memory experiences you will have. Keeping your mind alive and enjoying life is the key to maintaining it. When you allow the Holy Spirit (Sixth sense) to guide you through life, your memory bank will over-flow with the Fruits of God's spirit. There will be no desire to shut down.

I've heard people say, "I wish the world would just stop turning and let me off." Be careful what you ask for.

Touch: To exercise touch is simple: touch things. Enjoy the texture. Appreciate the sensation you feel from touching it; every object has a differ-ent sensation.   The sensations are so intricate that you can recognize different objects by merely holding them in your hand. An orange might be a ball until you feel the little bumps that make up its skin.

If you've been hurt by something you've touched before, your memory response will warn you. Hot or cold may remind you of danger. A rough piece of wood could remind you of a splinter.

A baby's smooth cheek will give you a soothing feeling that conjures up an emotional response of love.

Gently touching others will comfort you and connect you to them. A hug brings a warm sensation to both parties. A hug is the only gift you can give someone else and get the same thing in return.

I could go on and on with my experiences with touch but the best thing to do is just start doing it. Take a few minutes out of every day and experience your own sensations with touch. Do your own exercises; you have a memory bank just waiting to be revealed.

<u>Sight</u>: We see many things with our sight, but when you exercise, try using all of your eye to see. Use your peripheral vision as well. See the whole picture. Look from side to side as you do and take in more of the view. Try not to miss anything. Don't just glance at something, see everything. Fill your memory with beauty. Take a picture with your mind. This is what they call Kodak moments. You have taken in the sight so well that your memory can conjure it up any time you want to.

When you watch television, try to see everything in the room and still hear what is being said. This adds details to your memory bank. You will find you can recall much more of the program if you have more details.

In the fifth grade, our teacher asked us if anyone had seen the movie *Cinderella.* When several raised their hands, including me, she asked if anyone would like to tell the story. I said, "I would."

She said, "Just tell as much as you can remember, it doesn't matter if you leave anything out."

I stood up and told the story from beginning to end. When I sat down, she exhaustedly proclaimed, "Shirley you really need to learn to condense."

Disappointed, I said, "You said to tell everything I remembered."

Sighing, she said, "Yes I did, but you really need to leave some things out that aren't important."

I remember wondering what that would be. It wasn't until I was older that I understood what she meant. All I knew at the time was that she didn't like the way I told the story.

Your mind can store as much memory as you want it to, and if it is pleasant, you will want to recall every detail. Maybe the reason we don't use our brains to capacity is because we aren't storing good memory responses. When our minds store responses that have had a bad emotional effect on us, we push them as far back in our memory as we can. We'll start protecting our senses from such contacts again, in order to preserve our emotions. When we've had too many of these responses we'll shut down. That's when depression seeps in. Many times we push them as far back in our memory as we can, in hopes that it will never resurface. As soon as something bad happens again, it does.

With this fast-paced world, our sight often stores things we aren't fully aware of until it resurfaces. Even though we have the option to close our eye lids, many times we aren't quick enough. Just a glimpse of something bad or evil is enough to store a negative response in our brains. It is very important to censor what we put in our minds through our sight. Fear and anger can intermingle from something you see and cause an emotional overload creating anxiety. Your response is to hide, run or fight back, with no certainty of any of them. One thing is certain, if you don't have many positive responses stored in your memory, you will not have positive results in your life.

An enjoyable exercise you can do with your eyes is to find a place that is exceptionally pretty and take mental notes of everything you see. The trees, flowers, grass, birds singing, and squirrels playing. Just take in the beauty of God's creation. Let your mind clear and just watch and enjoy everything you see and hear. Allow God to consume your every thought, get in His presence. Just as we dump the cookies from our computer, we need to dump the spam the world has thrown at us. I just allow God to clear it all out and recharge my mind.

Another exercise you can do is go outside your house and look inside through the window. Pretend it is the first time you have seen inside. Look at everything as though you were a stranger looking in. When we are inside we take everything for granted; when you are outside looking in you are trying to see as much as you can. It truly does look different.

Also try to visualize how someone else would perceive your house.

Hearing: This, along with sight, are the two senses that we can't totally control. Just as we see things we don't always want to see, we hear things that we don't want to hear. We may tell our brains not to listen and try shutting it down, but we are not always successful. Especially if someone gets in your face yelling. The only way to not hear them is to walk far enough away so that you are no longer in hearing distance.

Hearing gives life to moving and still objects. When we are only able to see, we don't know exactly what is going on. We have to guess from their movement what is happening. Hearing takes away the confusion.

Deaf people have to rely on repetitive responses stored in the brain to know what is taking place. If it is something new, they will be confused or anxious until someone can show them in sign language what is going on. Their other senses can't explain what is going on so they have to rely on someone else to explain.

To exercise your hearing, you should turn down your television or music a couple of notches, until you can still hear it. When you have done this for a short period of time, your mind responds to the lower volume and your hearing will get better. We turn things up because we want to drown out other noises or we don't want to have to strain to hear something. What we are doing is becoming lazy.

When we don't use our senses to their capacity we stop using brain cells and cause them to dissipate.

It has been proven that loud noises over a period of time can destroy the ear drum and cause a loss of hearing. Maybe we destroyed the brain cells that contained the hearing responses we once had when we no longer concentrated on trying to hear.

Wives joke and say husbands have selective hearing. They'll say things like, "He can hear things when he wants to but let me say something to him. and he can't hear a thing." We all have selective hearing. If we don't want to hear someone we tune them out. I've discussed this earlier and how dangerous it can be.

Wives, when husbands don't want to listen to us, they simply don't want to hear what we have to say. Instead of telling us, and putting us on a rampage, they head off arguments by not listening. Maybe we should condense it down for them so they aren't so quick to shut us down, or try to make it more interesting to them. If we don't simplify unimportant conversations, then they won't be there when we truly need them to listen.

Men love us, they just don't want to listen to us when we go off on an emotional rampage. Talking is a verbal response to our emotions and men just aren't as emotional as we are.

The suggestions I have made may sound too simple to work. But we aren't aware of how we abused our senses until we start using them properly. You actually realize what you have been missing. Life becomes more vivid when we use our senses as God intended them to be used, and when we let the Holy Spirit guide us, we have more contentment with life.

I'm reminded of a joke were a man goes to heaven and St. Peter is showing him around the Mansion and he sees a door that is shut and tries to open it. When he discovers it is locked he asks St. Peter, "What is in there?"

St. Peter says, "You don't want to know."

"Yes I do. I want to see everything Heaven has to offer," says the man.

So St. Peter opens the door and the room has wall to wall shelves full of boxes.

"What are all those boxes?" the man asks.

St. Peter sadly says, "Those are all the gifts God wanted to give you while you were on earth but you never asked for them."

Not enjoying your senses as God intends for you to is just like the joke, you will miss out on all the gifts He wants to give you. So <u>smell</u>, <u>taste</u>, <u>touch</u>, <u>see</u> and <u>hear</u> all that you can and put positive responses in your mind. Not only will you enjoy them once, but you will be able to pull up those memories and enjoy them over and over again. There is so much of life that is beautiful and good if you take the time to enjoy it.

There are two responses we have to our senses that shut us down. *"I can't,"* and *"I don't want to."*

How many times have you had the opportunity to do something different and you didn't because your response was, I can't? If your response to your senses is I can't, then your mind will not do anything. It freezes us in place and no matter how much encouragement you get from others, if you have told your mind, "I can't", then you will not be able to.

When I was growing up, my mom and dad told me I could do anything I put my mind to. So I thought *'Wow, I can do anything.'* Because I could put my mind to everything, I had an open canvas and anything was possible. That was the best news I ever received in my young life.

The reason we tell ourselves we can't is because we are afraid of something. Afraid to get hurt, afraid of being laughed at or just simply afraid of failing.

I use to have a sign in my office that read:

If you begin doing something believing you are going to fail, and you fail; which have you done, failed or succeeded?

When you try new things, you should never worry about failing. Everything you accomplish is more than you once did or knew.

When I was a manager, I would tell my employees that when they set goals for themselves, to also set themselves a reward. Because only they knew how hard they worked for that goal, so they are the only ones who could reward themselves appropriately. Then if they almost made their goal, they could still reward themselves.

Many times we work extremely hard to reach a goal and when we succeed, the reward doesn't compensate all we went through. We feel let down.

Cheated somehow. In our minds, winning is going to bring an explosion of confetti with bands marching and everyone cheering. When that doesn't happen we are disappointed. No one really cares when you reach your goal or you win, except maybe the person that got you to do it. Even though you get the reward that was promised, you somehow think it wasn't enough. So reward yourself.

Remember, you can do anything you put your mind to. Put a lasting memory response in your mind: "I can."

"I don't want to": As I get older I find that "my want to" doesn't work as well as it used to. We can put our senses on a standstill by simply thinking, I don't want to.

I was surprised to discover how often those four words came to my mind. I can talk myself out of stopping somewhere after work in a matter of minutes:

"I don't want to drive over there."
"I don't want to get out of the car."
"I don't want to have to find a parking space."
"I don't want to walk a long distance to get in the store."
"I don't want to fight the crowd."
"I don't want to stand in line to check out."
"I don't want to spend money anyway."

My senses shut down and before I know it my car is headed home. I could give you a million examples of the "I don't want to" syndrome, but I'm sure you know what I'm talking about.

What I do now is work myself up to doing things. I call it gearing up. If I have said I would do something and I start wishing I hadn't, I turn it around and start thinking of the positive. How much I'm going to enjoy it. How nice it will be to be with my friends. The fun I will have. What it will mean to the person to whom I promised I'd be there. I stop thinking about myself and think about what I can do for others. Life isn't just about me, it's about caring and loving others as well. The more love you give others, the more you get back.

Sometimes, when I really don't want to do something but I need to, instead of thinking of all the reasons why I don't want to go, I just focus on getting dressed and going. No thinking, I just do it. But I keep a positive attitude that I will enjoy it after I get there.

If you do anything with a negative attitude you will not enjoy it. Furthermore, the people around you won't enjoy you either.

Instead of saying, "I don't want to," say "I want to," and see how it changes your attitude. Instead of your mind shutting down, a light bulb will come on and your response will be, "I can do that." It will turn your mundane, boring existence into an exciting and enjoyable life. A whole new world will be opened unto you if you put yourself out there and do something different. Don't let life pass you by and don't let fear control you.

Studies have shown that the best way to get over your fears is to face them head on. When we do this our mind will be full of responses that say, "I can do anything." Instead of hiding, you'll find yourself saying, "Bring it on."

There are individuals who stay frustrated because they can't do what other people do. The reason for this is they have never tried. Or if they tried once and failed, they never try again. So they have no memory responses in their mind that says they can.

People that are multi-talented are that way because they have mastered failure in those areas. To be good at something, you have to have a desire to be good at it.

A professional basketball player didn't just pick up a ball one day and say, "I'm good at this." He picked it up and used it until he was good at it. Now his mind knows he can do it because he has multiple memory responses in his mind that says he can.

People are always asking me if there is anything I can't do. I say, "What I can't do, I don't do. That way I am good at everything I do." (That's my little joke.)

You can only do things well if you put your mind to it. Instead of saying, "I can't," say "I can," until you truly can.

Say the words out loud so your ears can hear it. "I can" is such a positive statement and it will leave your mind with an empowering emotional response that will make you feel you can conquer the world. (With the sixth sense, Holy Spirit, you can.)

Life is full of new experiences and because of our senses we can do anything that we have a desire to do. Don't shut down your mind by saying, "I can't."

Remember the child in you and the excitement of learning something new. Broaden your horizons and let your mind enjoy the wonderful sensation of doing something new in life. Just remember to allow the Holy Spirit to guide you. God doesn't want to suppress you, He wants you to enjoy life through His eyes. See the world as He intended you to. Just stop suppressing God by saying, "I can't" or "I don't want to."

CHAPTER TEN

The Dark Hole of Depression

"I am the vine. You are the branches. Whosoever abides in me and I in him, he it is that bears much fruit, for apart from me you can do nothing."

John 15:5 KJV

Depression is a state of mind many of us have had, some more so than others. Many times we don't realize we have it until it is too late to do anything about it. I want to explain how we get to the point that we don't feel anything at all, and how depression takes over our lives and shuts down the proper function of our senses.

God is light and the devil is darkness. Put your hands together as tight as you can; when we are one with God, this is where we belong. Move your left hand away from your right hand. When we get caught up in 'self' we start moving away from God. We are no longer one with Him. Move away again and the light becomes dim. As you move farther and farther the darkness begins to engulf you; we are so far away from God that we can no longer see His light. We are in total darkness. The devil has control.

That is what people in a deep depression talk about when they say they feel like they are in a deep dark hole of despair. They feel that way because they are. They are so far removed from God, and so caught up in 'self,' they have to have someone bring them the light. Their senses no longer respond because they have isolated themselves from God. Their senses shut down.

Let me say though that it is easy to get caught up in self when you are trying to figure out what is happening to you. You begin to analyze your emotions trying to figure out what is making you feel the way you are. You try to make sense of what you're feeling and pretty soon all your thoughts are about 'me, me, me.'

There are many other issues in life that can cause you to get into a state of depression, even as a Christian. Health, loneliness, family problems, relationship failures, stress, and the death of someone we love are some of the experiences you may have throughout life.

When you are confronted with any one of these problems you will go into an emotional overload. When you have a loss, you will feel like a part of yourself is missing. Some psychiatrists describe it as a hole in your life.

When this occurs you have to find something

that will fill that hole. Just make sure you fill it with something good from God that will add to your life. Do not just grasp for anything to try and fill that hollow spot.

The more you grasp for things that don't bring joy to your life, the more that hole will get bigger and bigger. One day you will wake up and find yourself in such a deep hole of despair you are unable to get out of it without help.

I have fought depression for many years, especially since my brain tumor, because one of the medications I take causes it.

I'm a very upbeat person and I didn't know what to do about the depression at first. I couldn't figure out what was causing the negativity in my life when I had so much positive going on.

I learned to channel that negativity by helping others. It kept me from thinking about myself too much. It also made me feel good and gave me a purpose.

The worse my depression got, the more I helped others. (The biggest mistake I was making is that the Holy Spirit was not guiding me.)

I started helping several people at a time which took up all my free time. I became drained, and my mind became unable to function properly. I was physically and mentally exhausted. My senses were not in balance.

I became a giver and never received anything in return. I was a caretaker and I ran into people that just wanted me or anyone else to take care of them. The more I did for them the more they let me do. I became their crutch. (People who are needy will never allow you to be both their crutches because they want to remain in control.)

They wanted me to do for them the things they didn't want to do. Many times I did this unwillingly, which does not store a good memory response in your mind. (It certainly doesn't help depression.)

People who use you to be their crutch will never appreciate you, and will leave you in more despair than when you started. The hole you try to fill gets bigger and you begin to feel used up. When they see you are no longer any use to them they will move on to the next person, leaving you with a feeling of failure.

My problem is I have a hard time saying "no" to anyone. I had to learn I could only help others over and over until it started destroying me and then I had to let it go. I became cynical and felt everyone was out to use me. I developed the attitude that you can only help people if they are willing to help themselves. I started isolating myself from people because they seemed to drain me of my joy and the contentment I had in life.

For years I didn't have any pictures of people in my house. They were all landscapes. Pretty pictures that soothed me.

One day a friend of mine said, "Why don't you have any pictures of people anywhere?"

I thought about it for a moment and simply said, "Because people hurt you."

The very essence of who I was, was being

drained from me without my knowing it until it was too late. The hole I was filling by helping others began to engulf me. I found myself inside the hole and not knowing how to get out. I read my Bible and talked to God but was losing connection with others.

I began fearing people, afraid they would take what little bit of life I had left.

I felt like I was juggling my life and I knew the devil was throwing in thoughts that weren't correct, but I couldn't drop it from my juggling because I was afraid of dropping everything.

I tried to recharge my mind but I had no positive emotions coming in.

It is impossible to live a happy, healthy life by always giving and never getting anything in return.

Out of self-preservation I isolated myself from others, not only shutting down my sense of hearing but my sense of touch as well. I was shutting down two very important parts of life. I wasn't connecting with anyone except God. Or so I thought.

The thing is, when you stop using your senses as God intended you to do, you start loving from a distance. You don't allow anyone to get close to you, even God, because your senses begin to shut down and you don't feel His presence and don't want to be around anyone.

Remember our senses are our way of sharing everything we do in life with God. If we don't have God in our life, we don't have contentment.

That is why it is so important to use our senses in unison with God so He can keep us charged and filled with His Spirit when necessary.

On those instances that you feel drained and completely used up, you must find a quiet place where you can meditate upon God. (Let Him dump the cookies as I have explained earlier.) God will restore you and fill you, so you can carry on through life's struggles again.

Taste was the sense I used more than any of the senses because when I felt lonely, or unloved, unimportant, or unhappy, I rewarded myself with food. It made me happy. (Remember happiness is fleeting.) So I found myself rewarding myself over and over again (addiction).

People become addicted to food because it makes them happy at the moment. A few hours later they become sad, so they go back to the thing that made them happy, food.

If this is the only sense you are using, it becomes programed in your memory bank as the one thing that makes you happy, so you find yourself eating all the time even though you are not hungry. It becomes your total source of happiness.

Using one sense more and shutting down others causes an imbalance in the functioning of our minds and our responses become chaotic.

Emotions take over your life and you become afraid to move because movement might awaken a feeling you don't want.

Hiding seems to be the only way to keep control of unwanted emotions. You don't want to deal with anything or anyone because you can't. (Remember I said earlier I can't will freeze the mind.) No movement whatsoever is all you desire.

When your senses are locked down, the mind is locked down as well.

When you shut out the things around you and the rest of the world, your senses are no longer able to trigger the mind to function.

Details are hard for you to follow and comprehend, because you have no purpose, and therefore no need. You have no desire to do anything.

Details cause anxiety and with anxiety comes fear, so when someone wants you to do something specific you find it hard to follow their instructions and retreat further into yourself.

The devil loves it when you are afraid of something because he is able to take a strong hold of your mind through your emotions. Emotional overload is why you shut down in the first place; if he can continue that process, you will never come out of the darkness of despair.

To get out of this state of mind you must seek the Holy Spirit by praying and reading your Bible, and just listen. Psalm 46:10 says, *"Be still and know that I am God."*

Start trying to do projects that you feel you can't. Just a little at a time and let the Holy Spirit help you. It doesn't matter that you don't finish at first; what you are doing is waking up your mind. As you continue to try, it will get easier and easier. It took you awhile to get in that dark hole of despair; it will take awhile to awaken your mind.

You have told your mind 'I can't' for so long that you have lost the ability of knowing the details to a project.

At first your mind will be functioning in slow motion, but just take it one step at a time. Don't try to rush anything because this will cause you to get anxious and you will panic and your mind will instantly shut down.

Don't worry about how long it is taking you to do a project; the important thing is remembering the details. Write them down and if you feel you have left something out tap into the Holy Spirit that is always there and ready to help you.

This will take an enormous amount of concentration at first if you are very deep in the depression, but if you keep trying your mind will store positive responses and replace the negative responses that shut it down in the first place. Each detail you master becomes a milestone and you start awakening the parts of your mind that you allowed to get lazy by not using them during your depression. Windows will start opening and the darkness you have been in will soon be replaced by the light of God.

The anxiety will dissipate and the fear you have of trying will be replaced by peace. The kind of peace that can only come from God, and you will discover purpose again in your life.

The more projects you try to do, the more your mind will start functioning properly. 'I can' becomes a part of your vocabulary again and your senses become alive. You'll regain energy just as a computer does when you plug it in.

The only way to come out of the dark hole of despair is to start using your senses and connect to God.

CHAPTER ELEVEN

Fighting Depression & Alzeimer's

*I*n writing this chapter the thoughts and ideas I present are very personal and dear to my heart. When I was thirty-one my dynamic father, a man who had more common sense than anyone I have ever known, took his own life. He was a man who stressed there were consequences to everything you do in life. The one man who taught me that being strong was your best asset.

I just couldn't understand how a man like him could become so depressed that he would end it all with a gunshot to the head.

Shortly after that my sweet mother had a stroke and then a severe heart attack that left her with dementia. She died eighteen years later from Alzheimer's.

Fighting depression myself for many years,

and the fear that Alzheimer's might be hereditary, has motivated me to spend much time in prayer and study on the workings of the mind.

I kept asking myself how this horrible disease begins. What causes it to progress? At times it progresses quickly, but often it grows slowly. Why?

My Bible became my constant companion as I searched, trying to understand and deal with so many questions.

One day as I was reading in James, I came upon James 1:5 (KJV): *If any of you lack wisdom, let him ask God, that giveth to all men liberally, and upbraideth not; and it shall be given unto him.* In other words, if we seek knowledge, the Lord will give us the full wisdom we ask for. The Bible also tells us: *We have not, because we ask not.*

This book is the result of what God led me to discover and the amazing answers to my prayers.

It has been a long struggle, but God has taught me that by using our own senses we can overcome the devil's desire to steal our minds. If we understand what God had in mind when He gave us the wonderful gift of our "six" senses, so that our brains will grow with the knowledge He gives us and not deteriorate.

God gave us these gifts so we would continue to grow closer to Him and to experience the best of life on earth. We must put God in control of the one thing we are most afraid of losing, <u>OUR MINDS</u>.

Depression along with Alzheimer's is a disease that is quickly growing in our society. It can strike even the very young.

Strokes and heart attacks can also destroy the mind, and as I said earlier, I am not a doctor and can't give you any information to control these illnesses, other than prayer. God is always in control.

What I have observed with my Dad is, depression starts out as a state of mind, and can quickly progress into a terrible disease that shuts down the mind and body. It isolates us from the rest of the world; even though others may be in the same room, we retreat deeper and deeper into ourselves.

You learned from the earlier chapters how depression sneaks up on you and can progress into something that you will have to have help with to regain your health.

God brought me out of depression, and gave me the answers on how to recover. The key is God and keeping a balance of your senses. With God in charge, deterioration of the mind can be arrested. I am no longer depressed and I no longer get that sinking feeling that warns me it is coming.

God started making me aware of my senses to counteract the darkness that I was in. Hearing was the first sense God taught me how to properly use.

God made me aware of my sense of hearing by constantly telling me to be quiet and listen. At first I thought He meant to listen to Him, then I realized He also wanted me to listen to everything around me.

When people spoke, He reminded me to listen. Slowly but surely I understood what He was trying to teach me. He was making me aware of my sense of hearing and how to enjoy it.

I began to listen to people without talking. Just listened to what they had to say. It connected me with them on a more personal level.

Learning to communicate with others is an important part of life. Listening to what they have to say should be pretty basic, but surprisingly enough, people have forgotten how to listen properly. They love to talk but they have not mastered the art of how to listen. Here are five basic rules to being a good listener:

1. <u>Be attentive.</u>

Look them in the eye and concentrate on what the other person has to say. Don't look away or let your eyes wander; that is a perfect indication you are not listening. Learn to enjoy what people have to say. It is a rare gift that will bring you pleasure as well as the person you are listening to. Do not underestimate its power. Do not deprive yourself of the joy you will get from it, either.

2. <u>Show that you are listening.</u>

Unless you show people that you are listening, they will soon stop abruptly and lose interest in talking to you. You'll miss out on the really juicy information people will reveal when they are comfortable with you.

Your body language is a huge part of showing people you are listening. Have a relaxed open stance, don't shuffle from one foot to the other. Make eye contact, nod your head in agreement or disagreement. Prod them with questions from time to time, being careful to not take over the conversation. Reflect back or echo what they are saying occasionally. Check what they are saying, "Treated you badly? In what way?"

3. <u>Check Understanding.</u>

Show them you are on the same wavelength and are truly understanding what they are saying by agreeing with them or asking questions. Give them feedback from time to time, but as I said earlier don't take over the conversation with a situation of your own. There is nothing worse than having someone tell their own story when you are trying to tell yours. Try to empathize with them and if you can't at least sympathize with them.

4. <u>Be slow to pass judgement.</u>

Many people need to confide in someone that they feel they can trust. If you are quick to pass judgement or even appear to be passing judgement with your body language, they will shut down on you in an instant. Sometimes it is important to disagree with someone but don't do it in a way that will condemn them. Say something like, "I'm not sure I would have done it that way." Or, "Maybe you could do this instead."

5. <u>Use silence appropriately.</u>

It is very difficult to talk to someone when they are talking at the same time. Listen; silence shows acceptance and creates intimacy. People have a greater love for someone who will listen to them instead of interrupting them every time they start to talk. Some things are so important or shocking that the best response is an understanding silence.

As you can see, listening is a fine art. Something that takes practice. But it is most appreciated.

I found myself enjoying people again and am no longer hiding from them.

I found that with the Holy Spirit, (six sense) I was truly enjoying people and their uniqueness. Their stories were interesting and I felt joy, something that had been lacking for such a long time.

If you're not used to listening to others, it takes a lot of practice, but it is one of the most rewarding things you'll do in life.

I remember laughing one day and thinking, *when was the last time I enjoyed laughing?* It was such a wonderful sound to my ears and I suddenly felt I was coming alive again.

I began tasting my food and enjoying the texture, smell and essence of what I was eating, and I honored God for the abundance of it all. I not only thanked God for all that He had given me but invited Him to dine with me.

I took time to smell everything. I connected with God on a new level because in my busy life,

I barely took time to look at anything, let alone to smell it.

I stopped watching television programs that brought me fear, anger and disgust. I searched for programs that had good morals and gave me positive responses to life and allowed God to be a part of everything I did.

I stopped playing regular radio stations at work, and brought Christian CD's to play instead. It not only makes me happy to listen to the old Christian songs, but it has made my customers happy as well.

I am continuing to learn more and more every day about what God had in mind for us with our senses. He is teaching me to take control of my life, and be more dependent upon Him.

I don't just <u>touch</u>, <u>taste</u>, <u>smell</u>, <u>hear</u> and <u>see</u>, I have a depth to my life I never knew was possible. Everything in life is in 3D.

Reading the Bible is such a wonderful experience, because everything I read jumps right out at me. I have learned to meditate upon God and listen to Him as He talks to me. I don't allow worry and troubles of the world to destroy me. I am learning everything is about Him and not me.

By being obedient to God my life has far more meaning than I ever thought possible. I am learning to die to 'self' more and more every day, and my relationship with God is becoming stronger and stronger. Luke 9:23 KJV: *And He (Jesus) said to them all, if any man will come after me, let him deny himself, and take up his cross daily, and follow me.*

Filling your senses with God is the only way to

die to 'self' and stay in complete balance with Him.

I hope from reading this book you have learned the importance of the proper uses of your senses to give you positive Godly responses to your life.

Too much negativity will shut down the mind completely and this book is to help detour Alzheimer's. Once you have it, I don't believe you can come back from it because of the destruction of the brain cells. But I do believe you can help your loved ones who do have Alzheimer's by getting them to use their senses and staying connected to God.

You must have God's help because He never intended for us to go through life without Him.

Keep connected to God and don't isolate yourself from other people and use your senses in alliance with God and this earth will be a more enjoyable place to be.

When you greet people from your heart to theirs, all your senses will reflect God.

Scripture Found
Throughout the Text

For God has not given us the spirit of fear, but of power, and of love, and of a sound mind.

Behold, I stand at the door and knock, if any man hear my voice, and open the door, I will come in to him, and will Sup with him, and he with me.

That they may be one; as thou, Father, art in me, and I in thee, that they also may be one in us: that the world may believe that thou hast sent me.

I am the light of the world; he who follows Me will not walk in darkness, but will have the light of life.

Now then, stand still see this great thing The Lord is about to do before your eyes!

My sheep listen to my voice; I know them, they follow me.

It is better to live in the corner of the roof than share a house with a contentious woman.

For God so loved the world, that he gave his only begotten Son, that whosoever believeth in Him should not perish, but have everlasting life. (17) For God sent not His son into the world to condemn the world; but that the world through Him might be saved.

For in many things we offend all. If any man offend not in word, the same is a perfect man, and is able to bridle the whole body.

But the tongue can no man tame; it is an unruly evil, full of deadly poison.

The fruit of righteousness is sown in peace of them that make peace.

For if any man be a hearer of the word, and not a doer, he is like unto a man beholding his natural face in a glass: (24) For he beholdeth himself; and goeth his way, and straightway forgetteth what manner of man he was.

Greater is He that is in you, than he that is in the world.

Do not let any unwholesome talk come out of your mouths, but only what is helpful for building others up according to their needs, that it may benefit those who listen.

And if one prevail against him, two shall withstand him; and a threefold cord is not quickly broken.

A merry heart doeth good like a medicine, but a broken spirit drieth the bone.

I am the vine. You are the branches. Whosoever abided in me and I in him, he it is that bears much fruit, for apart from me you can do nothing.

Be still and know that I am God.

If any of you lack wisdom, let him ask God, that giveth to all men liberally, and upbraideth not; and it shall be given unto him.

And He (Jesus) said to them all, if any man will come after me, let him deny himself, and take up his cross daily, and follow me.

Bible Study Questions
(Important questions to ask yourself)

Before you can start the process of healing it is important for you to know what the devil is binding you with. Find out if there is something in your past that you just can't seem to let go of. Something you feel guilty or ashamed for and the devil just won't let you get past it.

Many times, the things that bind us are not because we haven't asked God for forgiveness and He not forgiven us. The real truth is we can't forgive ourselves so we punish ourselves, feeling we deserve to be punished.

For your first assignment, look over these questions and answer them to the best of your ability.

These questions will help you get to the core of your problem, and once you get rid of it and turn it over to God, you can start using your senses to connect with Him as He intended.

Maybe you don't want to answer the questions in a group, that's okay, just answer them on a separate sheet of paper for yourself. The important thing is to get it out and get over it.

Note: These questions are for the things we allow the devil to bind us with. It is in no way abusive situations that have been forced on you by someone else. You may need professional help, if you are not able to completely give it to God and allow Him to bring you to the light. The process of reforming positive responses in your mind, that will get rid of negative responses, will take more intense therapy.

1. Is there something in your past that you are ashamed of and can't seem to let go?

2. Is there something in your life you regret not doing and you can't stop thinking about it?

3. Do you feel you are not worthy of forgiveness? Explain why.

4. Have you asked God for forgiveness and you know He has forgiven you, but you can't forgive yourself? Explain why.

5. Are you afraid if others knew your secret that they would look down on you?

The great thing about God is once you have asked for forgiveness and He forgives you, you need no further validation from anyone. He is the great 'I Am,' the only one we must answer to.

Confession is good for the soul, but that doesn't mean that anyone, besides God, is going to help you. Now, if you know confessing something in the past will help someone else, then if you have the courage to do so, go ahead.

Once you have honestly answered these questions and God is in control of your life, you can use my book to wake up your senses and learn to have positive responses stored in your mind. The Holy Spirit will lead you out of isolation and you will start connecting with people and the world around you.

1. What are your five senses?

____

____

____

2. Which of your senses do you feel is most important to you? _____________________

____

____

3. What do your senses do? _____________

____

____

____

____

____

4. Are you aware of each of your senses and do you use them properly? ______________________________
____
____
____
____

5. Does your mind control what you do in life?
____
____
____
____

6. Are you aware of any of your senses being shut down? Explain.
____
____
____
____
____

7. Can you identify what may have caused those senses to shut down, so you can avoid those circumstances in the future?
____
____
____
____
____

8. Do you store positive reactions from your senses in your mind?

____

____

____

____

____

9. Do you allow the Holy Spirit to guide your senses or do you struggle to relinquish control?

____

____

____

____

10. Are you willing to use your senses to connect with God and stop living your life on an emotional roller coaster?

____

____

____

____

____

NOTES

A word from
the Author

Depression is a devastating disease that can creep into your mind and destroy the strong as well as the weak.

The last seven years have been a struggle for me, and I'm not sure if it was triggered by the medication I take since the brain surgery, or the fact that God was showing me the answer to the question I had asked Him, or both.

After my mother's death, I was determined to get an answer from God about what was causing Alzheimer's, and spent many grueling hours praying and talking to Him about it.

I have learned over the years that many times when we ask God a question, to get the answer we have to experience it. If He only answered the question, we would not have the empathy required to help others.

After taking care of my mother for eighteen years with dementia and then her later dying with Alzheimer's, I was determined to find out what causes it.

When I started my own Beauty Shop thirteen

years ago, I decided to cater to Senior Citizens. I have loved older people all my life and enjoy the wisdom they have to share. They are my family and many of them are like mothers to me.

I have asked many questions of people who have taken care of family members with Alzheimer's and have seen some of my clients deteriorate from it. But it wasn't until I went through depression myself did God start showing me answers.

After writing this book and sharing with you the things God taught me during the year and half I spent writing it, I feel that God has been getting me ready for this all my life.

The brain has always fascinated me, and after the brain tumor, it became a necessity to monitor it. The near photographic memory I had before was no longer there.

The tumor was located on the pituitary gland, and to get all of it they had to remove the gland as well. The pituitary gland controls all of the endocrine glands in the body. So basically, I no longer had a filter for my emotions. When I was excited, I was extremely excited. Sad, I was extremely sad. Happy, I was extremely happy. I blamed the extreme emotions on the medication I had to take for my hormones.

Toning down your emotions when they are at their extreme takes a lot of practice. Many times, I felt sad for no reason. Over time I learned to channel that emotion to a positive state of mind. So, I have been basically doing many of the things I described in the book ever since the brain surgery.

Six months after my mother died, five of my ladies died. Not only did it bring back the sadness I felt when mother died but it threw my emotions into a tail spin. At times my mind shut down.

That's when I started doing what I call 'projects' to channel my emotions and sort them out, one by one. I painted rooms in my house, one right after the other. Painted murals on walls. Came up with designs for my back yard and did anything I could to stay busy.

My friends were surprised at all the things I got done and voiced that fact to me many times. What they didn't realize was, I was fighting to keep my mind working properly. I had to use my senses when I did my 'projects,' but more importantly, the results made me feel closer to God.

At the time I didn't know my senses were helping me hang onto my mind. I wasn't sure what was happening to me, I tried everything I could think of to not be depressed.

Every time I almost came out of the depression, another one of my ladies would die. I was constantly grieving and I just couldn't get out of the dark hole I was in.

I left the large church I had attended for many years and starting going to a much smaller church. I had no idea why I was there but I was sure God had sent me there for a reason.

Shortly after I was there, the Pastor and his

wife lost their oldest son in a car accident.

During the grieving process they went through, he preached and taught us the things God was teaching them. As they progressed along, I began to understand what was going on in my life. I was in constant mourning.

It wasn't until our Pastor began to heal that I began to let go of the grief I felt each time one of my ladies died.

From the continual grieving, I had developed the 'me syndrome', because I was constantly trying to figure out what was wrong with me. As I began to heal I realized everything wasn't about me, it was about God.

My ladies who died were all Christians so I knew they were in heaven, but what I was grieving was, my loss. The fact that I would never be able to share anything with them again.

I found myself asking God how much loss can one person take without losing their mind? At times I felt myself actually shut down. I found it hard to concentrate on anything.

One of my clients, a friend, was in a car wreck and she asked me if I would come to her house and fix her hair. Of course, I did. While there I explained to her that I was having a hard time coming out of the depression I was in. I told her I would get so close, but just couldn't get free of it.

My friend is a great prayer warrior and she laid hands on me and prayed for me to be released of the depression and that I would have the answer to what was binding and holding me down before I got home from her place.

As soon as I got in the car and started driving the five miles to my house I said aloud, "Okay, God I am in agreement with Donna that you are going to tell me what is binding me and keeping me in depression."

God spoke to my heart and said, "You are angry!"

Shocked, I said, "Lord, I'm not angry with you."

He said, "You are not angry with me, you are angry with yourself."

I said, "What am I angry about?"

He said, "Think back."

I said, "Is it because Mother dying of Alzheimer's?"

He said, "No. Think back."

I thought for a moment and said, "Was it when I had the brain tumor?"

"Yes, but go further back."

My mind went back to when I had my first son.

My husband and I were stationed in Germany, with the Army, and I was in hospital having Shawn, my oldest son.

Back then they gave me Twilight to put me out because I had to have a caesarian birth. Then they gave me a shot to bring me out of the anesthetic.

My blood pressure went down to 60/10 and I was not coming out of the anesthetic. The doctor told my husband, sister and brother-in-law that was there in the room with me not to let me go to sleep, that I wouldn't come out of it.

I remember being so cold and shaking, and when I shut my eyes I didn't shake.

They shook me several times but I just wanted to sleep. Then suddenly I saw this beautiful meadow that was so green I can't find the words to describe it. Further down was a huge valley with a large beautiful tree in front of it. Behind the tree from the valley was a tremendous beam of light radiating towards the sky.

I started walking towards the light and the closer I got, I felt a peace go right through me. The more I walked the more peace I felt.

Then I heard my sister's voice say, "Shirley, come back!"

I kept walking, because I wanted more of the peace I was feeling.

I heard my brother-in-law's voice say, "Shirley, come back!"

I kept walking and then I heard my husband's voice say, "Shirley don't leave me!"

I stopped and turned around and when I looked at him, he was yelling, "Shirley, come back, don't leave me! Please, don't leave me!"

I started walking back and when I woke up, I could hardly breathe. My husband was holding me in his arms so tightly saying, "Shirley, don't leave me! Please don't leave me!"

I thought for a minute after recalling that beautiful experience and said, "I remember that Lord, but how is that making me angry?"

He showed me that since that time when anything went wrong in my marriage and life I became angrier and angrier because I had come back and not gone on to heaven.

Then when faced with death once more when I had the brain tumor I felt that peace again when I talked to the Lord the evening before the surgery. I said, "Lord, I am so tired of all this hurt and pain in my life, I just want to go feel that peace forever."

Suddenly, I felt little tingles go from my feet to the top of my head and the Lord showed me it was the lost souls of the earth. (Possibly the people I would come in contact with.) With total remission I said, "Lord if I can help one person be saved, then I am willing to stay."

Then God showed me that each time one of my ladies died, the devil would bind me with regret that I had chosen to stay. I became angrier and angrier that I couldn't go with them and feel the peace they must be feeling now.

The shop I had established was for the elderly

and I thought since I had almost died twice, I could help them die. The great thing about God is that through them, He was giving me a purpose to live.

When I got home, I went into my home office and the Lord said, "Look up senses on the computer."

I did, and when I read that your senses control the way you perceive life a whole new world opened up to me. God showed me it wasn't my mind that made me do crazy things. It was what I was doing with my senses. My mind was just where all my responses were stored.

That's when God made me aware of my senses and how they should be used properly in a balance with the Holy Spirit as my guide, thus the result of this book.

The devil loves to use regret and anger to bind you and isolate you from people and God.

'If only I had,' are the four words the devil loves to control your mind with, because it will keep you in the past and you will be unable to move forward.

His biggest lie is that isolation will protect you from the cruelty of this world. When he throws in fear (which is the root of anger) he uses it to encourage you to hide. This causes you to fall deeper and deeper into despair and darkness. Before you know it, you are in a hole you can't get out of without help.

When you relinquish regret, anger and fear to God, He brings you out of the darkness and fills you with light and hope.

The dark hole of despair becomes a room made

of windows with light coming in from every direction.

"You are set free!"

I learned to let go of self and just let God take charge of my mind and life.

God gave me answers and showed me I had the power within myself, with His help of the Holy Spirit, to overcome anything in life.

www.ingramcontent.com/pod-product-compliance
Lightning Source LLC
Chambersburg PA
CBHW060934050726
47592CB00003B/956